Ethical Admonition
in the Epistle of Jude

Studies in Biblical Literature

Hemchand Gossai
General Editor

Vol. 4

PETER LANG
New York • Washington, D.C./Baltimore • Boston
Bern • Frankfurt am Main • Berlin • Vienna • Paris

Kenneth R. Lyle, Jr.

Ethical Admonition
in the Epistle of Jude

PETER LANG
New York • Washington, D.C./Baltimore • Boston
Bern • Frankfurt am Main • Berlin • Vienna • Paris

Library of Congress Cataloging-in-Publication Data

Lyle, Kenneth R.
Ethical admonition in the Epistle of Jude / Kenneth R. Lyle, Jr.
p. cm. — (Studies in biblical literature; v. 4)
Includes bibliographical references and index.
1. Bible, N.T. Jude—Criticism, interpretation, etc. I. Title. II. Series.
BS2815.2.L95   227'.9706—dc21   97-38142
ISBN 0-8204-3838-3
ISSN 1089-0645

Die Deutsche Bibliothek-CIP-Einheitsaufnahme

Lyle, Kenneth R.:
Ethical admonition in the epistle of Jude / Kenneth R. Lyle, jr.
–New York; Washington, D.C./Baltimore; Boston; Bern;
Frankfurt am Main; Berlin; Vienna; Paris: Lang.
(Studies in biblical literature; Vol. 4)
ISBN 0-8204-3838-3

Cover design by James F. Brisson.

The paper in this book meets the guidelines for permanence and durability
of the Committee on Production Guidelines for Book Longevity
of the Council of Library Resources.

© 1998 Peter Lang Publishing, Inc., New York

Printed in the United States of America.

To Anita, Walker, and Emma

Acknowledgments

I wish to thank several individuals who have helped to bring about the completion of this book. Thanks first to Peter Lang Publishing for their interest in this project. I am particularly indebted to Hemchand Gossai who provided helpful corrections to the manuscript. Any errors that remain are solely because of my inattention to detail.

I am forever grateful for the encouragement and attention that I have received from Dr. Glen Stassen. I am thankful for his suggestions about how to approach the analysis of ethical admonition, and I will take up his charge to "spread the word."

Thanks also to Bill Carrell and Tim Crawford, my colleagues at Bluefield College, for their support and encouragement. A special thanks to Rita Blevins for her help in producing the manuscript.

Table of Contents

List of Figures

Editor's Preface

More than ever the horizons in biblical literature are being expanded beyond that which is immediately imagined; important new methodological, theological, and hermeneutical directions are being explored, often resulting in significant contributions to the world of biblical scholarship. It is an exciting time for the academy as engagement in biblical studies continues to be heightened.

This series seeks to make available to scholars and institutions, scholarship of a high order which will make a significant contribution to the ongoing biblical discourse. This series includes established and innovative directions, covering general and particular areas in biblical study. For every volume considered for this series, we ask the question as to whether it will push the horizons of biblical scholarship. The answer must be *yes* for inclusion.

In this volume, Kenneth Lyle has explored carefully the ethical admonitions in the Epistle of Jude. He has not only provided a significant overview of the relevant literature, but has taken the discussion into new and thoughtful directions. Professor Lyle's interest goes beyond the academic, as he pursues a course which he believes has been overlooked in scholarship and which he argues is essential for the church.

This volume will undoubtedly shed new light on a neglected aspect of the study of the book of Jude. Part of what makes this volume important is that it will provide insights into the ongoing discourse within the church regarding a framework for biblical ethics. The horizon has been expanded.

Hemchand Gossai
General Editor

Preface

My interest in the Epistle of Jude began as a matter of circumstance and has continued because of an ever increasing interest in this unusual and unique letter. In my first semester of Ph.D. study, Dr. Gerald Borchert asked that I review Richard Bauckham's commentary on Jude and 2 Peter for his Non-Pauline Literature seminar. In addition I wrote a paper for that seminar entitled *The Ecclesiology of Jude and 2 Peter.* In subsequent semesters, I continued to research and write about the Epistle of Jude, completing grammatical studies of Jude and 2 Peter, and a paper on *The Use of the Old Testament in Jude and 2 Peter.*

At the same time, I pursued an interest in the issues surrounding the synoptic use of the phrase ὁ υἱος τοῦ ἀνθρώπου. For Dr. George R. Beasley-Murray's seminar on the Synoptic Gospels, I wrote an introductory paper entitled *The Son of Man in the Synoptic Gospels.* In a later semester, I produced a more limited treatment on *The Coming of the Son of Man in Mark 8:38, 13:26-27, and 14:62.*

The unlikely juxtaposition of these two lines of investigation leads to this proposal. Jude's use of *1 Enoch* 1:9 in vv. 14-15 where "the Lord comes with his tens of thousands of holy ones" is strikingly similar to those passages in the synoptic gospels where the Son of Man comes with angels (Mark 8:38; Matt. 16:27, 25:31; Luke 9:26, et al.) While Richard Bauckham makes this point, he only just touches upon it, and he does not give enough attention to the possible links between the two streams of thought. My speculation about how these two patterns of thought relate to one another helped to foster the thesis that the Epistle of Jude might well represent the concerns of the early Christian community.

In the fall of 1993, I was privileged to attend Regent's Park College at Oxford University to complete my university study. At Regent's, under the direction of Dr. Larry J. Kreitzer, I was able to do research into the background, and interpretation of the Epistle of Jude. In addition, I was able to attend many of the University seminars. Of particular interest was a lecture given to the New Testament Graduate Seminar by Margaret Barker. Barker is a Cambridge educated scholar, and a prolific writer on the Old Testament, and intertestamental literature. Among her works are *The Older Testament* (1987), and *The Lost Prophet: The Book of Enoch and Its Influence on Christianity* (1988). In her remarks to the seminar, Barker suggested that if we are to know anything of Palestinian Jewish Christianity, or the religious milieu in which Jesus conducted his ministry we must look to the non-Pauline texts—books like James, the Apocalypse, and Jude! This assertion strikes me as absolutely correct, and resonates with my suspicion that the Epistle of Jude occupies a transitional position between the religious milieu in which Jesus worked, and the preaching and teaching of the early Christian community.

While all of these lines of thought cannot possibly be drawn together within the scope of this investigation, it is possible to begin approaching the problem by establishing a fresh understanding of the primary purpose and message of the Epistle of Jude. I contend that the Epistle's concern with ethical admonition and, in particular, the admonition to be merciful is inherently linked with the redemptive action of God in Christ. Moreover, Jude offers a window (albeit a small one) into how the early Christian community interpreted the Christ event in light of their apocalyptic worldview. This worldview understands the implications of the Christ event both in terms of eschatological judgment, but also for the admonition to live out the Christian life.

Finally I wish to thank several individuals for their significant contribution and encouragement during the preparation of this project. First, to the members of my Committee of Instruction I offer my heartfelt thanks for their guidance, instruction, and patience. Thank-you to Dr. Gerald Borchert who assigned a paper on The Epistle of Jude in my first graduate seminar, and who has continued to offer help and encouragement as a mentor and friend. Thank-you to Dr. James Blevins who allowed further investigation and reflection on the significance of the Epistle of Jude in his Greek seminar, and who demonstrated that teaching is the greatest role an actor can play. Thank-you to Dr. David Garland, who first instilled a love of the New Testament in me, and who then helped me to understand the importance of balance and priority in life and work. In addition, I owe a tremendous debt of gratitude to Dr. Glenn Stassen, who suggested his model as a possible means of understanding the ethical admonition in the Epistle of Jude.

To my fellow graduate students, I say thank-you for your patience and encouragement even in the face of my preoccupation with Jude. Thanks to the members of the New Testament Colloquium, both past and present who suffered my endless references to Jude. In particular I am grateful for the friendship of Alan Tomlinson, Jack Painter, Paul Smith, and Gary Poe.

To my parents I offer a heart-felt thanks for their support and love. In a very real sense this book is a tribute to the love of study and reading which my parents gave to me. To my children, Walker and Emma, I give both my thanks for all the joys they bring me, and an apology for the times when I allowed my study and writing to interfere with the far more important task of being a parent. Their contribution to my learning and development is substantially more significant than my independent endeavors. May they know the joy of being "kept and called" by Jesus Christ.

Finally, I offer a far too inadequate expression of thanks and love for the support and help of my wife Anita. Without her constant encouragement, sympathy, and even pestering, this project never would have reached completion. She deserves more praise and thanksgiving than I can possibly produce, but that won't stop me from trying!

"Now to him who is able to keep you from falling and to present you before his glory without fault and with unspeakable joy, to the only God, our Savior, be glory and majesty, power and authority, through Jesus Christ our Lord, before time was, now, and in all ages to come, Amen."

Chapter One

Introduction

The Epistle of Jude has been called "The Most Neglected Book in the New Testament."[1] This short, powerful letter is most often cited for its concluding doxology, its unusual use of pseudepigraphic material, its relation to Second Peter, and its strong polemical stance; less attention, however, has been given to the relative position of Jude's epistle in the development of the teaching and preaching of the early Christian community. One suspects this lack of attention is due primarily to the epistle's unusual composition, its brevity, its citation of non-canonical writings, and its presumed "early Catholic" status among the books of the New Testament.[2]

The observation that New Testament scholarship has essentially bypassed the study of Jude is not revolutionary.[3] While there have been several recent efforts to deal with the Epistle of Jude in great detail, the lack of attention given this small but interesting letter by both the scholarly community and more importantly the church, stands at the heart of the problem that this monograph seeks to address.[4]

Purpose and Rationale

While the Epistle of Jude occupies a small place in the New Testament, it contains interesting and potentially informative data concerning the early Christian community. This study suggests that the key to understanding the role of the Epistle of Jude in the early Christian community lies in a proper understanding of the ethical admonitions that are at the heart of Jude's letter.

Previous studies of the Epistle of Jude concentrate primarily on "secondary" issues of authorship, dating, provenance, and character; however, there is less emphasis given to the "primary" message of the book that centers on ethical behavior within the Christian community. Moreover, because of certain methodological presuppositions that have driven the scholarly approach to Jude, little regard has been given to the potentially important position of the Epistle of Jude in the developing theological and ethical teachings of the early Christian community.[5] While recent studies have focused on the rhetorical or literary structure, the historical setting, or the sociological significance of the letter there has yet to be an effort to concentrate solely on the ethical mandates that are the focus of Jude's message.[6] Moreover, there has been no significant effort to relate Jude's ethical admonitions to the teaching, preaching, or theological development of the early Christian community.

Methodological Considerations

It is the contention of this study that the ethical stance taken by the author of the Epistle of Jude represents not the latest developments in the teaching of the early church, but rather the earliest strands of New Testament teaching regarding proper behavior within the Christian community.[7] To that end, certain methodological concerns must be addressed. From these concerns, particular questions can be formulated which will help to drive the investigation that follows.

First, there is the problem of uncertainty. The Epistles of Jude and 2 Peter, like no other books in the New Testament, are plagued with the problem of uncertainty. This uncertainty is intensified by the very attempts to remove it with speculation about the time, place, or author of the writing, which tend to be crippled by their circular arguments. The question of date is dependent upon one's assertion about the author. The question of authorship is dependent on an assertion about the place and destination of writing; and all these issues influence the interpretation of the nature and purpose of the letters.[8] Anton Vögtle illustrates the interpretive maneuvers attempted by some scholars in order to avoid the problem of uncertainty. In his discussion of the origin, destination and authorship of the letter, Vögtle correctly points out that many scholars remain either silent on these critical issues, or they roughly accommodate all suggestions. Vögtle cites one scholar who suggests that "Jude, after the death of James, could have felt responsible in a particular way for the Jewish Christians in Palestine, Syria, and Egypt...perhaps his influence with Jewish Christians in Asia Minor extended even to Rome."[9]

The second concern, which grows out of the first, is the nature and character of the Epistle of Jude. Previous interpreters have allowed certain methodological presuppositions to drive the force of their investigation of the Epistle of Jude. Chief among these is the presumption that Jude, along with 2 Peter, is grouped together into an artificial category of New Testament writings with the all encompassing title "the Catholic Epistles."[10] Recent studies have helped to clear away the fog surrounding the designation of Jude and 2 Peter as "early Catholic"; however, the problem of interpreting the message of Jude in particular still requires our attention.[11]

Finally, Jude's use of pseudepigrapha and preoccupation with apocalyptic imagery requires that some attention be given to the nature of Jude's apocalyptic worldview. Jude's working within the rubric of apocalyptic in order to bring about a particular didactic goal is well founded.[12] Less certain, however, is the nature of that particular teaching goal. What does our understanding of apocalyptic tell us about the nature and purpose of Jude's letter?

Three primary concerns have been outlined, and they give rise to three essential questions for our understanding of the primary message of the Epistle of Jude. First, what can be said with certainty concerning the Epistle of Jude, and what can be assumed as a working presupposition? Second, what has previous scholarship said about the primary message of the Epistle of Jude, and what influence does that scholarship have on a contemporary interpretation of Jude's message? Finally, how does our understanding of apocalyptic inform our interpretation of the message of the Epistle of Jude? These primary questions, and the secondary issues that they raise will be the driving force behind this investigation.

The Plan of the Investigation

The answering of three primary questions does not suggest a particular methodology, or structure; however, it is necessary to project a plan of investigation that will guide the process.[13] To that end, the remainder of chapter one is given over to establishing what can be said with relative certainty about the Epistle of Jude. The scope of the investigation does not permit an in depth discussion, but in an effort to establish some working presuppositions, the remainder of chapter one offers a brief discussion of character, date, authorship, relationship to 2 Peter, destination, and purpose of the Epistle of Jude.

Chapter two is an attempt to provide a model for dealing effectively with the interpretation of Jude's ethical admonitions throughout history. This model should demonstrate how previous interpretations have shaped and possibly distorted our current understanding of the purpose and message of the letter. Since no established model for evaluating the ethic of a biblical text suggests itself, the first task is to establish such a model. Glen Stassen's cogent description of Critical Variables for evaluating Christian Social Ethics provides the foundation for a model of evaluating how Jude's ethical admonitions have been previously understood.[14] Stassen's model suggests four primary variables or criteria for evaluating Christian social ethics: the mode of moral discourse, the ground of meaning, the perception of the situation, and the existence of loyalties, interests, and trusts. With slight modification these criteria can be applied to how previous scholars have understood Jude's ethical admonitions, and the strengths and weaknesses of those positions can be evaluated.

Chapter three evaluates the manner in which Jude's ethical admonitions have been interpreted throughout history. It is essentially a limited *Forschungsgeschichte* that focuses on a particular element of interpretation, which employs the critical variables outlined in chapter two in its analysis.

Chapter four builds on the analysis of chapter three and suggests that a proper understanding of Jude's ethic requires an approach that integrates all of the critical variables affecting the interpretation of ethical argument. This study suggests that the essential framework for this integrative task is found in our understanding of apocalyptic writing, and the apocalyptic worldview shared by Jude and Jude's audience. To that end, chapter four seeks to establish apocalyptic as the key to understanding Jude's ethical admonitions. Relying on the significant work of Christopher Rowland, the essay argues that Jude is characterized by that apocalyptic worldview that gives equal emphasis both to eschatological events, and—more significantly—to the living of everyday life within the Christian community.[15] The monograph seeks to ground the interpretation of Jude's ethical admonitions in a proper understanding of apocalyptic and an apocalyptic worldview. This will allow the creation of a model for evaluating Jude's ethical admonition which integrates all of the critical variables for evaluating ethical admonition and diminishes none.

Chapter five takes the model for evaluation of ethical admonition, and offers an analysis of Jude's argument, and general purpose in writing the letter. Equal emphasis is placed on Jude's admonitions against ethical misbehavior and for a proper understanding of God's mercy. While the primary purpose of this exercise is to establish the content and background for Jude's ethical admonitions, a secondary result will be the testing of a new evaluative model with the Epistle of Jude providing suitable and manageable subject matter. Finally, the study offers some conclusions regarding the significance of the present research for our better understanding of the preaching and teaching of the early Christian community.

Introductory Issues in the Epistle of Jude

While an exhaustive examination of the critical issues surrounding the study of the Epistle of Jude is not warranted, the proposed avenue of research requires that some preliminary groundwork be done to set the parameters for further study. These working presuppositions will help to focus the study on the primary issue of the ethical message of the Epistle of Jude, while acknowledging the difficulty of dealing with a biblical text that offers few hints as to its origin.[16]

In most general commentaries on the Epistle of Jude, issues of date, authorship, provenance, and the relationship to Second Peter dominate the discussion. Presumptions about a single issue often determine the conclusions about the remaining questions.[17] This is particularly true of nineteenth century scholarship, where often an unfounded determination of the "heresy" Jude is arguing against led to unwarranted speculation about the identity of the author, date, and origin of the writing. While primary attention is given these issues, much of what is offered by modern scholarship is a simple reiteration of the predominant views of nineteenth and early twentieth century scholars.[18] The only conclusion that can be drawn from this level of consistency is that the trap of circular argument knows no century.

Few scholars have moved beyond the conventional interpretation of the Epistle of Jude as a "catholic" letter directed to the whole church and offering a word of general exhortation. Even very recent treatments of the nature of the early Christian community draw on Jude and 2 Peter as examples of the "developing" Church, and draw a negative conclusion about the value of these letters for modern readers.[19] This study does not take issue with the assertion that Jude and 2 Peter represent the early development of the Christian community, but particularly in the case of Jude, holds open the question of whether there is evidenced in this letter a greater sense of ecclesiastical development.

Recently, Richard Bauckham has provided significant guidance with his contributions to the study of the Epistle of Jude. Bauckham's work is ground breaking and exhaustive at points. His work provides a strong foundation for further study, yet it does not prohibit further investigation into the primary message of the epistle. Using Bauckham's significant contribution as a framework, some brief guiding statements are offered concerning the character of the letter, the date of the writing, the author, the relationship to 2 Peter, its destination, and primary purpose. These presuppositions provide for a more thorough examination of Jude's ethical admonitions.

Character of the Letter

At the foundation of scholarly debate about the character of the Epistle of Jude is the question of the understanding of Jude's worldview. Scholarship has offered two dominant views concerning Jude's worldview: Jude is either representative of "early Catholicism,"[20] or it was written within a Jewish Christian apocalyptic context.[21] The predominance of the "early Catholic" position taken by many modern scholars can be attributed to the influential work of Ernst Käsemann.[22] Although Käsemann wrote primarily about 2 Peter, the close relationship between the two letters allowed the "early Catholic" classification to influence the study of the Epistle of Jude. The influence of Käsemann is articulated by Heiligenthal who argues that with his theological classifications and appraisals of Jude, Käsemann determined the direction of a large part of the Protestant research after him.[23]

These two broad descriptions—"early Catholic," or Jewish Christian apocalyptic—establish the extremes in the debate over how scholarship has interpreted the character of the Epistle of Jude; yet they also represent the meeting place where many interpreters understand Jude functioning as a transitional document between Christianity as a Jewish sect and Christianity as a distinct religion.

Bauckham's most significant achievement is his discussion of the nature and character of the Epistle of Jude. Bauckham rejects the designation "early Catholic" for both Jude and 2 Peter and successfully demonstrates that in the case of Jude, the early Catholic designation is particularly inaccurate.[24] Bauckham outlines the evidence for the designation "early Catholic" as follows: (1) these letters supposedly exhibit a greater level of ecclesiastical development, (2) they have lost the parousia hope, and (3) the gospel has crystallized into set forms.[25] Bauckham successfully refutes the notion that these three criteria apply to the Epistle of Jude.

Ecclesiastical officials are not addressed, but rather "…the whole community, who all enjoy the inspiration of the Spirit in charismatic prayer (v. 20) and are all responsible for upholding the Gospel (v. 3)."[26] There is no call to yield to the authority of an elder, a bishop, or even a pastor, but rather it is argued that authority belongs to τὸν μόνον δεσπότην καὶ κύριον ἡμῶν ᾿Ιησοῦν Χριστὸν (v.4).

There is no evident loss of the Parousia hope. The writer of Jude makes no attempt to explain any delay in the return of the Lord. Unlike the situation reflected in 2 Peter, where the opponents argue: Ποῦ ἐστιν ἡ ἐπαγγελία τῆς παρουσίας αὐτοῦ; ἀφ᾽ ἧς γὰρ οἱ πατέρας ἐκοιμήθησαν, πάντα οὕτως διαμένει ἀπ᾽ ἀρχῆς κτίσεως (3:4), the troublemakers in Jude are not portrayed as ridiculing the expected return of Christ. On the contrary Vögtle claims that the whole thrust of the letter hinges on the fact that at the height of Jude's argument, the author seizes on a christological interpretation of the judgment prophecy in *1 Enoch* 1:9 where the faithful along with an escort of angels and the established Christ come to judge the opponents with their own words and actions.[27] The certainty of the coming judgment and its consequences for both the wicked and the righteous is the driving force behind the letter. The hope of the Parousia has not faded. Rather, it stands as part of the foundation for the ethical admonitions in the letter.

The argument about "crystallized forms" of the gospel hangs on the interpretation of "faith" in v. 3. It is frequently argued that the phrase τῇ ἅπαξ παραδοθείσῃ τοῖς ἁγίος πίστει (v.3) demands a doctrinal view of πίστις, as a once for all delivered body of teaching.[28] Bauckham argues that to make "faith" in verse three "…refer to a fixed body of orthodox doctrine…is a misinterpretation of v. 3, which refers simply to the gospel itself, not to any formalized and unalterable 'rule of faith.'"[29] The "faith" question is essential for a proper understanding of the primary message of the Epistle of Jude, and therefore it must be examined at every point in this brief review of critical issues influencing study of the Epistle of Jude.

Beyond the above three criteria that are often imposed on the Epistle of Jude, Bauckham argues that this additional judgment about the nature of the argument in the Epistle of Jude has led to its classification as an "early

Catholic" letter, namely the assertion that "…Jude's letter is violently polemical…" offering denunciation rather than theological argument.[30] Jude's polemical character has often been overstated. Otto Pfleiderer's assertion that Jude "…contains a brief but vigorous condemnation of certain false teachers…" has been consistently maintained in one form or another over the last century and a half.[31] The letter has been characterized as "a firebrand,"[32] "a straight forward polemical tract,"[33] a *"lettre de combat,"*[34] "violent polemic,"[35] and an *"antihäretisches Flugblatt."*[36] The distinctive character of Jude's polemical stance, linked with presuppositions about date, and the nature of "faith" is often held out as the reason for Jude's "early Catholic" designation.[37]

Recent scholarly treatments have shown, however, that the characterization of Jude as "mere denunciation," or "violent polemic" "…exaggerates the relative importance of the polemical section (vv. 4–19) in the letter."[38] Bauckham argues cogently that verses 4–19 comprise "a very careful piece of scriptural exegesis" intended to provide the background to the primary appeal of the letter found in verses 3, 20–23.[39] The strongly Jewish character of Jude's epistle has been consistently recognized, and Bauckham makes the well-received argument that Jude reflects apocalyptic Christianity with a particularly Jewish flavor. Bauckham points to the use of *1 Enoch*, the *Assumption of Moses*, the Hebrew Bible, pesher exegesis, the prominence of angelology, and "the emphasis on ethics rather than doctrine" as evidence for his conclusion.[40] Bauckham calls upon the work of Douglas Rowston who argues that Jude is consciously using the rubric of apocalyptic to turn back the antinomian trend that has grown out of a misunderstanding of Pauline teaching.[41] Rowston's argument is persuasive at many points, but Bauckham critiques and refines Rowston's thesis offering a helpful corrective by suggesting that Jude's use of apocalyptic is less self-conscious and more a result of the innate use of the prevailing worldview of both Jude and the audience.

Bauckham's articulation of Jude's apocalyptic Jewish Christian worldview demonstrated in the Epistle of Jude has been accepted by most scholars over the last decade; recently, however, there has been some critique of Bauckham's position. Emphasizing Bauckham's characterization of the problem facing Jude as primarily one of ethics, Vögtle demurs:

Considering this [Bauckham's] identification of the adversaries [antinomian libertines] it cannot surprise, that Bauckham emphasizes as always, the quarrel not between "orthodoxy and heresy in the faith, but around the relationship between the gospel and moral obligation" about "the moral implications of the gospel."[42]

Vögtle favors the position that the conflict represented in Jude is between orthodoxy and heresy, and clings to the "early Catholic" characterization of the Epistle of Jude.

The Epistle of Jude is understood to be either an example of "early Catholicism," or a product of apocalyptic Jewish Christianity. This study favors the latter position. Chapter two is an attempt to analyze how a precise determination of the nature and character of the letter is essential for a proper understanding of Jude's ethical admonitions.

Date

The broad range of dates proposed for the composition of the Epistle of Jude is perhaps greater than for any other book in the New Testament.[43] Guthrie states:

The fact that the suggestions of scholars regarding the date of writing vary between A.D. 60 and 140 is a sufficient reminder that much of the so-called evidence on this subject amounts to little more than guesses.[44]

Guthrie's assertion is a sobering reminder that many "conclusions" in biblical studies are founded on nothing more than a predisposition to a particular view of the nature and character of the text in question.

Internal evidence on which to base a sound judgment about the date of the letter is limited. Scholars who resonate with the "early Catholic" interpretation of the Epistle of Jude suggest that the citation of pseudepigraphic material (vv. 9, 14–15), the use of the "formulaic" phrases like ἡ κοινὴ ἡμῶν σωτηρίας (v. 3), ἡ ἅπαξ παραδοθείσῃ τοῖς ἁγίοις πίστις (v.3), ἡ ἁγιωτάτῃ ὑμων πίστις (v. 20), and the apparent passing of the apostolic age (v. 17) eliminates the possibility of an early date. Arguments about the date of the letter invariably center on the above concerns, and are

linked very closely with stated positions on authorship, character, relation to
2 Peter, and purpose. The danger of circular argumentation again becomes
apparent.

Most nineteenth-century treatments assume a late date for the letter
primarily because of a presumed "heresy," or a decision about the
pseudepigraphal authorship of the letter.[45] Modern treatments of the letter
successfully refute the late date for Jude, and make a strong case for a first
century date; yet even among that group of scholars who posit a first century
date for the Epistle of Jude, there is diversity of opinion regarding the question
of how early to date the letter.

The use of *1 Enoch* and *The Assumption of Moses* has led many scholars
to propose a later date because of a presumption about the availability of these
ancient sources. Recent studies have shown, however, that the portions of *1
Enoch* that are cited by Jude were readily available even before the first
century.[46] While less certain, the qualified conclusions about the date of *The
Assumption of Moses* place it in the early part of the first century.[47] Jude
certainly would have had access to these traditions. C. E. B. Cranfield argues
that while these writings were suspect in later centuries, they "...were highly
revered in the first century in the very circles in which members of the Lord's
family are likely to have moved."[48] The use of *1 Enoch* and *The Assumption
of Moses* in no way mandates a late date for the letter.

Concerning the argument that the Epistle of Jude contains "formulaic"
phrases (vv. 3, 20) which refer to an orthodox body of doctrine and therefore
point to a late date because of the required passing of time, Guthrie and
Bauckham have both convincingly stated that these phrases need not refer to
a set body of beliefs, but can equally refer to the more general expressions of
the gospel (Rom 6:17, Gal 1:23, Eph 4:13, Phil 1:27). Leaney argues that this
"faith" language "...implies that the Christian church has been in existence
long enough to become first settled in its teaching, and then to be influenced
by some men whose teaching is not only wrong, but evil and dangerous."[49]
Yet even scholars who hold to the "early Catholic" interpretation of Jude and
understand "faith" and "our common salvation" to refer to a set body of
doctrine have not found it necessary to postulate a late date for the letter.[50]

The so-called passing of the apostolic age that many scholars emphasize
in their interpretation of verse 17 reads too much into the text. Jude's
admonition to the readers of the letter, μνήσθητε τῶν ῥμάτων τῶν

προειρημένων ὑπὸ τῶν ἀποστόλων, need not refer to a long passing of time, but rather an interval that would allow the hearers of both the letter and the words of the apostles to make that vital recollection which Jude is admonishing.[51] Any assertion that verse 17 must in some way refer to a time when all the apostles have passed from the scene requires a leap of reasoning and association that is not present in the text.[52]

A final piece of internal evidence that has weighed in heavily on both sides of the issue is the author's self-designation as Ἰούδας Ἰησοῦ Χριστοῦ δοῦλος, ἀδελφὸς δὲ Ἰακώβου (v.1). The question of authorship significantly influences the issue of dating, and will be briefly examined in the discussion below.

External evidence for the date of the Epistle of Jude rests primarily on an understanding of its relationship to 2 Peter. Of the two letters, Jude is by far the better attested. It is mentioned in the Muratorian Canon (late 2nd century), by Clement of Alexandria (150–215), Tertullian (160–220), Origen (185–254), Eusebius (260–340) who calls it a "disputed book," and Jerome (342–420).[53] Yet Jude's greatest witness is 2 Peter, and the relationship between the two books dominates the discussion in many commentaries, articles, and monographs. In anticipation of the following discussion of this issue, it can be said that when the priority of 2 Peter is maintained its date becomes the *terminus pro quem* for speculation about the date of Jude. When the priority of Jude is maintained, 2 Peter becomes the *terminus ad quem*. Exact dating of the Epistle of Jude is not possible, but recent arguments favor a first century date. A brief discussion of both the identity of the author of Jude and the letter's relationship to 2 Peter may allow for a more precise presupposition about the date of the letter.

Authorship

If a first century dating for the Epistle of Jude is allowed, then a decision about the identification of the author of the letter may suggest a more specific date within the first century. The designation Ἰούδας Ἰησοῦ Χριστοῦ δοῦλος, ἀδελφος δὲ Ἰακώβου (v.1) offers several clues as to the identification of the author. The name Ἰούδας designates no less than six individuals in the New Testament. Two of these individuals may be excluded from consideration as authors of the letter. Judas Iscariot, the most prevalent Ἰούδας in the NT, and

Judas of Galilee (Acts 5:37) are both improbable choices for authorship. Matthew and Mark list Ἰούδας among the brothers of Jesus (Matt 13:55; Mark 6:3). Luke identifies ὁ Ἰούδας Ἰακώβου as one of the twelve disciples (Luke 6:16; Acts 1:13), and also places ὁ Ἰούδας in Damascus at the time of Paul's conversion (Acts 9:11). Finally, Acts 15 describes the efforts of Ἰούδαν τὸν καλούμενον Βαρσαββᾶν (vv. 22, 27, 32).

Except for Judas Iscariot, and the Judes of Acts 5:37 and 9:11, each of these individuals has been associated with the author of the letter of Jude.[54] The association of the letter with the Ἰούδας Ἰακώβου in Luke-Acts fails because the most natural meaning is "Jude, son of James" rather than "Jude, brother of James."[55] Most recent treatments of the Epistle of Jude favor the identification of the author as Jude, the brother of James, the brother of Jesus.[56] Ellis cogently argues that the author is the Ἰούδας of Acts 15. [57] Either of these positions—Jude, the brother of Jesus, or Jude of Acts 15—allows the possibility of an early date. Most scholars accept that Jude, the brother of Jesus is the intended author of the letter. There is, however, some question about whether the author is actually Jude, or a faithful disciple of Jude or James who is gaining authority for the writing by using the pseudonym Jude. For Heiligenthal the matter is closed, "Der pseudepigraphe Charakter de Jud wird nicht mehr bestritten."[58] Those who hold that Jude is a pseudonym do so invariably because of their decision about a late date for the writing of the letter that extends beyond the limits of the presumed lifetime of the actual Jude.[59]

If, however, an early date for the composition of Jude is accepted there is no compelling reason to reject Jude, the brother of Jesus as the author of the letter. The prime factor in favor of Jude as author is the simple observation that if Jude is a pseudonym, why choose so obscure a figure?[60]   Attempts to explain Jude as an appropriate pseudonym are often fraught with complex arguments. Vögtle suggests that the pseudepigraphal author knew of the death of James and chose Jude as a pseudonym because Jude had survived his brother and was still known at the turn of the century. This author then chose to add the title "brother of James" to set himself apart from others who might share the name Jude and to lend authority to his moral instruction.[61] It is possible that an individual knew of the death of James, and chose to use the name of his brother Jude, and was forced to add the title "brother of James" to insure proper identification. It is more reasonable to accept that a genuine

ʾΙούδας wrote on his own behalf and identified himself in relation to both his brother James, a leader in the Jerusalem church, and in proper deference to the Lord Jesus Christ.[62]

The only real argument against Jude as author of the letter is the unusual grasp of the Greek language that traditional scholarship argues could not be expected from a "Galilean villager."[63] Scholarship has shown that the influence of Greek language and culture in Palestine was far more pervasive than previously recognized, and there is no reason to reject Jude as the author simply because the letter betrays a grasp of Greek.[64] Bauckham argues that in addition to our increased knowledge about the influence of Greek language and culture in Palestine, there is nothing to suggest that Jude "…should not have deliberately improved his command of Greek to increase his effectiveness as a preacher." Further, Bauckham points out that "a wide vocabulary, which Jude has, is easier to acquire than a skill of literary style, where Jude's competence is less remarkable."[65]

Ellis's assertion that the author is to be associated with the ʾΙούδας of Acts 15 is compelling at many points. This identification allows for close association with James, knowledge and appreciation of Old Testament and Jewish apocryphal traditions, the ability to write with a good grasp of the Greek language, and a predisposition to argue against "…false teachers (and their diaspora adherents) opposed in the Jerusalem decree."[66] It should be noted, however, that each of these distinctives could apply equally to Jude, the real brother of James, the brother of Jesus. Moreover, as Bauckham argues, the Judas of Acts 15:

> …might be expected to distinguish himself from others of the same name by using his surname Barsabbas, rather than "brother of James," even if this can be taken to refer to spiritual fraternity.[67]

While dogmatic conclusions are not possible, the weight of evidence stands slightly in favor of Bauckham's articulation of the identification of the author, although Ellis's position is intriguing. As with all conclusions about critical issues in the Epistle of Jude caution should reign. This study favors the position that the author of the letter is Jude the brother of James, the brother of Jesus.

Relationship to 2 Peter

On the relationship between Jude and 2 Peter there is widespread scholarly consensus that Jude has priority over 2 Peter; a few scholars, however, who are anxious to maintain Petrine authorship of 2 Peter hold that Jude is copying and editing 2 Peter.[68] The various arguments surrounding the priority of Jude, the priority of 2 Peter, or the existence of a common source have been outlined on numerous occasions.[69]

In favor of the priority of Jude it is often argued that Jude is briefer and more spontaneous, suggesting a subsequent writer (e.g., 2 Peter) would tend to expand and revise. Some commentators have emphasized Jude's harsh tone, pointing to the abrupt change of direction in verses 3–4 and suggesting that the letter is "…struck off at white heat!"[70] Second Peter seems less abrupt, and less intense in its outright condemnation of the troublemakers in the community. Finally, it is argued that 2 Peter's omission of reference to *1 Enoch* and *The Assumption of Moses* suggests a more developed sense of canon.[71]

While most modern treatments of Jude and 2 Peter focus on the significant parallels between the two texts and speculate about where literary dependence lies, Jerome Neyrey points out that conclusions about priority are often predicated "…in a context of presuppositions and hypotheses."[72] Again the problem of circular argument becomes clear. A presumption about the character of Jude, e.g., violent polemic, drives the characterization of 2 Peter as being less harsh, and therefore secondary. The omission of Jewish traditions need not point to a higher view of canon, but only to a different historical situation. Arguments for the priority of Jude that emphasize 2 Peter's reordering of OT events, omission of pseudepigraphal writings, and expansion of Jude's argument fail to recognize that those arguments can be used to reach the opposite conclusion, namely that 2 Peter is prior to Jude.[73]

In the end, only two tentative assertions affect the decision of this study to presuppose the priority of Jude. First, is the conclusion that Jude 4–19 is "…a very careful piece of scriptural exegesis…."[74] As Watson states:

> It is easier to see how the author of 2 Peter could use the material of Jude 8c–18 to construct a less structured denunciation of the false teachers, than how Jude could utilize 2 Pet 2:10b–18 to construct a tightly woven argument

to show the sectarians were predicted in prophecy.[75]

The reworking of Jude's careful argument, for either theological, canonical, or situational reasons, suggests that 2 Peter follows Jude. Second, is the simple observation made by most proponents of the priority of Jude: If 2 Peter is prior, why write Jude at all?[76]

Beyond these two assertions, arguments for or against the priority of Jude or 2 Peter become fraught with difficulty. The limited evidence indicates that the priority of Jude can be presupposed with some confidence.

Destination

A problem which hampers discussion of the destination of the Epistle of Jude is its characterization as a "general" or circular letter.[77] Chase argues, however, that "...although the destination is not named in the Salutation, the situation with which the letter deals is too concrete to be universally applicable."[78] Even scholars who characterize Jude as a circular, or general letter proceed to argue from the perspective that Jude writes against a specific problem.[79]

J. A. T. Robinson's assertion that "while there are clues in James that point...to a Palestinian milieu, there is nothing in Jude that affords any hint of where the author is living" overstates the case.[80] While there is limited internal evidence, scholars have proposed numerous possibilities for the destination and location of the letter. Rome, Alexandria, Palestine, Syria, and Asia Minor have all been proposed.[81] Although each location has its strong supporters, the majority of scholars favor a Palestinian/Syrian destination.[82] Recently, however, Gunther has argued that "... associations with Syria and Palestine are superficial."[83] Yet, Jude's use of OT images, Jewish apocalyptic traditions, and identification with James clearly suggests a community under a heavy Jewish-Christian influence.

Scholars who hold that the letter was intended for a community outside Palestine, or Syria, point to Jude's good grasp of Greek, the "gnostic" nature of the problem the letter addresses, or the ethical libertinism of the opponents that points to a misunderstanding of Pauline theology.[84] These factors would suggest a post-Pauline, Diaspora community, in contact with pagan concepts and ideas. In short, the letter appears to address a community within a

Hellenistic Jewish context.

Until recently, these factors would have mitigated a location outside Palestine. Hengel has demonstrated, however, the "unqualified use of the term Hellenistic no longer produces clarity."[85] Hengel's presentation of the level of Hellenization that existed in Palestine, and even Jerusalem demonstrates that "there is hardly any doctrinal theme in the New Testament which could not also have been thought or taught in Palestine."[86] As a corollary, there is hardly any doctrinal or behavioral problem within the early church which could not have arisen in Jerusalem, or at least in Palestine. Such a situation would require the attention of a leader in the Jerusalem church—an individual like Jude.[87]

In the end, however, scholarship needs to take cognizance of Schelkle's conclusion that "Der Entstehungsort des Briefes wird sich nicht mit Sicherheit angeben lassen."[88] Indeed there are no "safe" answers to many of the critical issues surrounding the Epistle of Jude. Yet the increased understanding of the level of Hellenization within Palestine indicates that a destination within the Palestinian milieu is possible.

Purpose

Interpretations of Jude's purpose in writing are closely related to the critical issues which are briefly outlined above. Decisions about the character, date, and author of the letter influence the final decision about Jude's primary purpose. This study contends that Jude's purpose relates primarily to the ethical admonitions that are at the heart of the letter; therefore, a full discussion of the letter's purpose would bespeak the examination that follows; however, two summary observations are possible. First, judgments about the character of the letter shape conclusions about the purpose behind the writing of the letter. Second, no matter how scholars judge the character of the epistle, there is an overwhelming tendency to emphasize the negative or polemical aspects of Jude's letter to the exclusion of the more positive aspects of the ethical admonition that stands at the heart of the letter.

Scholars who characterize Jude as an example of "early Catholicism" maintain that Jude's purpose was to write a polemical defense of the faith. Traditional scholarship has focused on the apparent shift in mood between verses three and four. It is often argued that Jude had both an underlying and immediate reason for writing. Initially, the intention was to write about the shared salvation which Jude and the audience knew; but because of an outbreak of trouble in the community, Jude is moved to write this rather scathing attack on the troublemakers.[89]

Scholars who resonate with the Jewish-Christian apocalyptic character of the letter emphasize the "exegetical" middle section of the letter (vv. 4–19), and focus on the appeal in verses 3–4, 20–23.[90] The letter is intended to identify the character of the troublemakers, point out the certainty of their condemnation, and urge the faithful to remain so at all cost. While this assessment is closer to the mark, it suffers from the same basic flaw as the imposition of an "early Catholic" characterization on the letter.

Both "early Catholic" and apocalyptic interpretations of Jude tend to emphasize the negative thrust of the Epistle of Jude against something. Jude is almost exclusively characterized as a polemic, or exegetical argument against heresy, false teaching, or unethical behavior. Over against this monolithic characterization of Jude's purpose, this study seeks to establish the twofold thrust of Jude's ethical admonition that places equal emphasis on admonition against unethical behavior and for a proper understanding of God's mercy.[91]

Conclusion

The primary concern of this chapter is the question of what can be said with certainty, and what can be taken as a working presupposition when approaching the introductory issues affecting the study of the Epistle of Jude. This brief survey of the critical treatment of the character, date, author, relationship to 2 Peter, destination, and purpose of the letter demonstrates that there is in fact very little which can be said with certainty about the Epistle of Jude. However, the weight of evidence often allows for the establishment of sound presuppositions. Therefore, this investigation proceeds from the following framework. Jude, working in the decade between A.D. 50 and 60, writes to a specific community, most likely within Palestine, about a specific problem. Jude's use of Old Testament types, *1 Enoch*, and *The Assumption of Moses* betrays a Jewish-Christian apocalyptic context for the letter. The purpose of the letter is to argue the twofold thrust of the ethical admonition that stems from Jude's apocalyptic worldview.

This final point is really the driving force behind this investigation: a reevaluation of Jude's purpose in writing the letter based on an understanding of Jude's apocalyptic worldview. The following chapters attempt to demonstrate how previous scholarship has ignored or misappropriated the importance of Jude's apocalyptic worldview for a proper understanding of the ethical admonition in the letter. This tendency has kept scholarship and the church from a proper understanding of the twofold thrust of the ethical admonition in the Epistle of Jude. To that end, chapter two attempts to provide a model for dealing effectively with the interpretation of Jude's ethical admonitions throughout history. The model will help to demonstrate how an integrative approach to the interpretation of ethical argument and ethical admonition provides a more accurate analysis of Jude's message and purpose.

Chapter Two

A Model for the Interpretation of Jude's
Ethical Admonition

Having established some general working presuppositions, it remains to answer the second in our series of questions: What has previous scholarship said about Jude's ethical admonition and mode of ethical argument? Clearly the impact of previous scholarship on continuing interpretation of the Epistle of Jude is amplified because of the lack of internal evidence, and the tendency to accept prior conclusions as correct. This is particularly true of how scholarship has approached the critical issues dealt within chapter one.

To set the stage for a revised understanding of the primary message and purpose of the letter, it is necessary to understand how Jude's ethical stance has been interpreted in the past. Previous conclusions about the nature and purpose of Jude's ethic are often accepted without critical evaluation. The characterization of Jude as "mere denunciation," a strong polemical statement, or an "early Catholic" letter, distort the more positive aspects of Jude's ethical admonitions and mode of ethical argument. As has been demonstrated, these "conclusions" are often reached because scholars seize a particular emphasis, or presupposition and allow these factors to color the whole of their interpretation.

A proper understanding of Jude's primary concern with ethical admonition requires a clear understanding of the elements that comprise ethical admonition and ethical argument. What follows is an attempt to establish a model for understanding how Jude's ethical admonition and mode of ethical argument have been interpreted previously. In response to this study of how Jude's ethical position has been interpreted, the conclusion of this chapter offers a more integrated approach to understanding the ethical admonition and mode of ethical argument in the Epistle of Jude.

Critical Variables in Evaluating
Christian Social Ethics

The difficulty in undertaking a history of how Jude's ethical admonition has been interpreted is that the criteria for such an evaluation are not readily available to biblical scholarship. The categories "ethical admonition" and "mode of ethical argument" are not generally included in commentaries and monographs which deal with biblical texts. It is therefore necessary to establish the criteria by which the interpretation of an ethical stance can be identified and critiqued. The challenge is to establish criteria that are not arbitrary, which can be accepted as authentic scholarship, and offer genuine insight into the processes that drive ethical admonition and ethical argument.

Ethicists engage in evaluation and critique of ethical positions at the level of social and political policy decisions. Significant scholarly debate has produced various models for understanding "...the elements entailed in justifying a decision or a policy."[1] These models, whether secular or Christian, identify the primary presuppositions that influence judgments, arguments, conclusions, and responses to ethical questions. Glen Stassen has created a schema that distinguishes the major critical variables in evaluation of Christian social ethics. Stassen's model incorporates the critical variables that affect the nature and direction of ethical argument, and diagrams the relationships between those variables. Stassen articulates the importance of such a model:

> The need is to avoid the narrow vision that repeatedly stumbles into error and loses its way because it ignores major dimensions of ethical decision, ethical argument, and ethical character.[2]

Stassen's charge is one that should be taken up by biblical scholars who wish to understand how the ethical admonition and mode of ethical argument in a particular text have been previously interpreted, and how they should be interpreted.

The significance of Stassen's model is that it demonstrates how the various critical variables interact with one another in the ethical decision making process. The identification of interacting variables is the primary strength of Stassen's approach. More often than not, analysis of ethical argument focuses on a particular variable or factor. In like manner, biblical study often emphasizes one methodology, or presupposition over against others. With modification, Stassen's model provides biblical studies a window into how the ethical admonition of a particular text should be interpreted. At this point, however, caution should reign. Stassen's model is designed for interpreting contemporary ethical debate and decision making; any attempt to modify it for use in biblical studies should acknowledge that the model provides simply another avenue to approach the history of interpretation.

The four primary critical variables in Stassen's schema are: (1) the mode of moral discourse, (2) the ground of meaning, (3) the perception of the situation, and (4) loyalties, interests and trust.[3] How these variables interact in the decision making process determines the result in ethical debate. To use Stassen's words, these criteria are "like independent variables in the social sciences; they are the factors that shape the outcome of moral arguments."[4] The schematic relationship between the variables is depicted in the following diagram:

Critical Variables in Ethical Character and Decision Making[5]

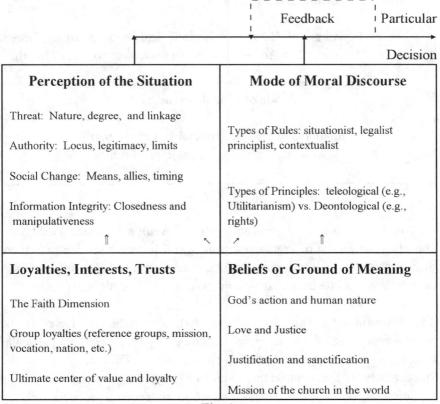

Perception of the Situation	Mode of Moral Discourse
Threat: Nature, degree, and linkage	Types of Rules: situationist, legalist principlist, contextualist
Authority: Locus, legitimacy, limits	
Social Change: Means, allies, timing	
Information Integrity: Closedness and manipulativeness	Types of Principles: teleological (e.g., Utilitarianism) vs. Deontological (e.g., rights)
Loyalties, Interests, Trusts	**Beliefs or Ground of Meaning**
The Faith Dimension	God's action and human nature
Group loyalties (reference groups, mission, vocation, nation, etc.)	Love and Justice
	Justification and sanctification
Ultimate center of value and loyalty	Mission of the church in the world

Fig. 1

Within each major category, Stassen delineates several determinative factors or variables that determine ethical argument and decision making. Moreover, the schematic seeks to describe the interrelationships among the four dimensions. The particular strength of Stassen's model is that it demands that analysis of ethical argument and ethical debate acknowledge and understand the significant relationships between the various dimensions. A brief description of Stassen's critical variables will allow a better understanding of his general framework, and will provide a foundation for establishing a modified version of the model for use in understanding how scholarship has interpreted ethical argument and admonition in the Epistle of Jude.

The Mode of Moral Discourse

The first quadrant of Stassen's schematic deals with the style of moral reasoning. This variable "…does not concern the *content* of ethics but the

Mode of Moral Discourse
Situationist, Legalist, Priniciplist, Contextualist Teleological Ethics v. Deontological Ethics

Fig. 2

logic of how one puts the ingredients together."[6] Within this category, Stassen classifies the nature of arguments with regard to how they are presented. Stassen describes the situationist, legalist, principlist, and contextualist. Each of these types is characterized by how the content of ethics is expressed.

The Situationist. Operating at the Particular Judgment Level is the Situationist. At this level of moral reasoning "…one speaks of a particular case, expressing a judgment but giving no reasons."[7] The emphasis is on the "particularity" of the situation that requires a judgment. To declare a specific act immoral, or to brand a particular group as incorrect, without offering substantive reasoning is an example of a particular judgment. For our understanding of how Jude's ethic has been interpreted, this category might be modified by asking: Does a particular scholar understand Jude as maintaining a particular judgment without offering support for such a judgment? Put more simply, does the particular scholar understand Jude to be a situationist?

The Legalist. Individuals who operate at the Moral Rules Level are classified by Stassen as Legalists. Unlike the Particular Judgment Level, at the Moral Rules Level reasons for the judgment are stated. The reasons do not arise out of "...a general principle...but a specific directive telling what to do in particular cases like the rule, 'Thou shalt not kill.'"[8] At this level community, or group dynamics play a significant role because "moral rules usually come from some community or institution to which a person belongs or from which he benefits."[9] Again, we might anticipate the direction of the model's modification. Does the interpretation present Jude offering specific rules for or against a particular judgment? Can Jude be properly interpreted as a "legalist?"

The Principlist. Those who operate at the Principles Level also provide reasons for their judgments. Here, however, there is an understanding that

> rules are based on reasons or general principles...the rule is a specific application of a more general principle which does not give specific direction for what to do but gives a reason for rules that do.[10]

Stassen cites the example of the principle of the sacredness of life which leads to a rule against murder. Debate about the nature of ethics occurs at the principles level, and Stassen distinguishes two broad approaches: (1) Teleological ethics, where the means is justified by positive consequences of the end, and (2) Deontological ethics, where rules, judgments and decisions are validated by reasonable assessments of proper conduct.[11] Adaptation to a new interpretive model would require analysis which identifies those scholars who acknowledge that Jude's argument flows out of established principles. Further, the model must determine whether those principles arise from validated assessments of proper conduct (the deontological approach), or from utilitarian methods of argument (the teleological approach).

The Contextualist. Stassen's final classification within the category Mode of Moral Discourse is the Contextualist. The Contextualist operates at the Level of Basic Beliefs, applying basic beliefs to each new situation. The emphasis at this level is on the response of individuals to new ethical dilemmas where the response is generated not by adherence to a rule, or a principle, but to the more basic level of beliefs that flow out of the individuals or groups foundational understanding of reality. Stassen argues for the superiority of the Contextualist position over against that of the situationist, the legalist, or the principlist. For Stassen, the superiority of contextualism is related specifically to the Christian context of ethical debate. For Christian ethics:

> The strength of contextualism is that it hears the biblical message at a profound level and does not reduce it to a book of proverbs announcing rules and principles. It speaks profoundly to the human situation from the richness and depth of Christian Faith, and avoids the closed and boxed-in rigidity of legalism.[12]

The Level of Basic Beliefs stands very close to the second quadrant in Stassen's schematic, the Ground of Meaning. This logical progression demonstrates how ethical arguments filter up from an individual, or group Ground of Meaning to the level of basic beliefs and eventually become established in principles, rules, and judgments.

The Ground of Meaning

The second and most significant quadrant in Stassen's schematic is called the Ground of Meaning. The Ground of Meaning variable operates from the initial supposition "…that several existential assumptions or questions are logically entailed by ethical thought, whether or not we operate from an explicitly religious framework."[13] Beyond the general existential framework for ethical thought, Stassen points to the "…confessional or specifically theological sense [in which] particular Christian teachings seek to answer these existential questions."[14] Stassen projects two primary questions that arise from this assertion: (1) Why should one act morally? or Why should one be convinced by a particular ethical argument? and (2) What is the normative ethical imperative, and how does one reconcile the disparity between that norm and the "realities of the fallen world?"[15]

Beliefs or Ground of Meaning

God's Action and Human Nature
Love and Justice
Justification and Sanctification
The Mission of the Church

Fig. 3

The Ground of Meaning variable has to do fundamentally with the motivation to ethics, the content of ethical obligation, the source of power or motivation to ethics, and the agent or channel of ethics. In the Christian context, the motivation to ethics stems from the Christian perception of God's action in human history. In response to the question "Why ought I be moral?," Stassen argues that "…the most important Christian loci are the doctrine of creation and human nature, and the shape and purpose of God's action in history."[16] The motivation to act ethically stems from God's creation of humanity in God's own image to be ethical and moral beings. Humanity should be ethical because God created humanity to be ethical.

The content of ethical obligation rises out of the human response to God's action. The content of ethics provides "…a way to handle discrepancy between the authority of ethical imperatives and the demand of worldly powers."[17] Stassen suggests the Christian concepts of love, justice, and particular Christian teachings (e.g., The Sermon on the Mount) as the specific content of obligation. The question of how one can function ethically relates to the source of power to perform ethical conduct. Stassen injects the categories of justification and sanctification at this point, dealing with the questions "what are we to be saved from, and what sort of goodness can we hope for?"[18]

The channel, or vehicle for ethical conduct is the concern of the final variable in the Ground of Meaning quadrant. Here, the essential question is "…what do you assume is the channel or vehicle through which goodness becomes effective in the world, especially in the face of conflict, change, and hope?"[19] From a secular position, the vehicle of effective goodness might be government policy, community action, or social activism. In the Christian context the primary channel or vehicle for effecting goodness is the Church, or community of believers.

Identification of the particular Ground of Meaning of an individual or group is essential for accurate analysis of their ethical stance. The Ground of Meaning quadrant interacts significantly with both the Mode of Moral Discourse, and with the third quadrant, the Perception of the Situation. Modification of the Ground of Meaning variable for use in the proposed evaluative model requires some determination about how Jude's ethical position has been interpreted with regard to the motivation to ethics, the content of ethics, the power to do ethics, and agent of ethics. For the Epistle of Jude, the resolution to these questions is related to how one interprets the author's particular worldview.

Perception of the Situation

The third quadrant of Stassen's schema deals with how an individual or group perceives a particular situation, or interprets data.[20] As there are four variables in the Ground of Meaning quadrant, Stassen also identifies

---

Perception of the Situation

Threat: Nature, Degree, and Linkage
Authority: Locus, Legitimacy, Limits
Social Change: Means, Allies, Timing
Information Integrity: Closedness and Manipulativeness

Fig. 4

four critical variables for analysis of how situations are perceived. Stassen argues:

There are more ways of perceiving the situation of decision than we usually imagine. An unthinking approach is simply to look at what appears to be going on or to read some research and then to accept the results uncritically.[21]

In an effort to qualify the various ways of perceiving the situation of decision Stassen posits the elements of threat, authority, social change, and information integrity and demonstrates how they interact in the process of interpreting and defining a particular situation.

Threat: Nature, Degree, and Linkage. Stassen argues that ethical perspective is significantly influenced by threat perception, and "…in turn, threat perception is heavily influenced by ground-of-meaning assumptions about human nature."[22] The nature of the threat refers to how the threat is qualified, the degree of the threat refers to how the threat is quantified, and linkage refers to how the threat is connected to other elements.[23] Modification of this variable for use in the proposed evaluative model would allow for analysis of how the perceived threat in the Epistle of Jude has been characterized and interpreted. It would necessarily question how the *nature* of the perceived threat has been described (e.g., false teaching or antinomian behavior); how the *degree* of the perceived threat has been interpreted (e.g., proto-gnosticism v. full-blown gnosticism); and how the *links* to other elements have been identified (e.g., links to "Pauline" language, the "heresy" identified in 2 Peter). In addition to analyzing how the nature, degree and linkage of the perceived threat have been interpreted, the model would have to allow some description of how these elements relate to the Ground of Meaning identified by the interpretation.

The Nature of Authority. The second critical variable in the Perception of the Situation quadrant is "…the nature of authority and its relation to the basic ground-of-meaning norm."[24] The location, legitimacy, and limits of authority are factors that influence this critical variable. Ultimately, the nature of authority stems from Ground of Meaning beliefs. Stassen argues that "in Christian terms, the authority question is related to the question of the principalities and powers."[25] How one relates to principalities and powers while still remaining grounded in the ethical norm of love and justice is the defining characteristic of the perceived nature of authority.

For the proposed evaluative model, the question of the nature of authority would relate primarily to (1) where the interpretation *locates* authority (e.g., faith as a body of doctrine), and (2) how the interpretation views the *legitimacy* and *limits* of authority. The interpretation of the perceived nature of authority is intrinsically linked to the interpretation of the ground of meaning, therefore, in the evaluative model it is also intrinsically linked to the question of the interpretation of Jude's worldview.

The View of Social Change. This variable is very closely connected to the Ground of Meaning variable which deals with vehicle or channel for ethical conduct. Its impact on the perception of the situation relates to how an individual or group determines who or what should be the agent of social change. In the secular context, this variable hinges on questions about the role and responsibility of government agencies, and social policy; in the Christian context, however, the view of social change "...is closely related to the mission of the church."[26] The content of this variable is made up of questions about the acceptable *means* of change, appropriate *allies* in the quest for change, and expected *timing* for change.

Understanding the relationship between the Ground of Meaning, and the perception of how social change should take place is vital for proper analysis of ethical positions. In like manner, the proposed evaluative model requires careful consideration of how Ground of Meaning affects the ethical admonitions, or changes, called for in the Epistle of Jude. The acceptable *means* of change called for (e.g., condemnation of false teachers), the appropriate *allies* suggested (e.g., church officials), and the expected *timing* of the admonitions (e.g., the question of eschatology), could be incorporated into the evaluative model in order to understand how these elements have been interpreted by previous scholarship.

The Information Integrity Variable. The final variable which impacts the Perception of the Situation quadrant is the information integrity variable. This variable deals primarily with the question of openness to other points of view, and the degree to which information related to the ethics of the situation is made open and unfettered. How information about a particular situation is "closed," or manipulated will influence how the situation is perceived.

In the proposed evaluative model, information integrity would relate to how the information about the ethical situation in Jude has been interpreted. The investigation would center on whether a particular interpretation understands the situation described in the letter as accurate or inaccurate. Does the interpretation see a specific situation in the description, or a general description of a widespread problem? Information integrity is influenced by the issue of pseudepigraphy, and the proposed location, or origin of the letter.

Loyalties, Interests, and Trusts

The fourth and final quadrant in Stassen's schematic deals with loyalties, interests, and trust. Stassen acknowledges that loyalty can be to

---

Loyalties, Interests, Trusts

The Faith Dimension
Group Loyalties
Ultimate Center of Value

Fig. 5

a particular *means* of achieving a specific goal, or to a particular person; but, he follows Potter in focusing on group loyalties and the ultimate center of value as pivotal for this dimension of ethical decision making.[27] Again, it is important to note that the Ground of Meaning affects both group loyalties, and the ultimate center of value. In fact, Stassen suggests:

> the study of loyalties is not a major additional task, but a matter of making explicit what one already has discovered in studying the other elements in an ethical argument.[28]

The Faith Dimension. How the question of "faith" is understood to derive from the Ground of Meaning dimension is an important factor in a proper understanding of the loyalties, interests, trust quadrant. While some have argued that the "faith dimension" should be subsumed to the Ground of Meaning quadrant, Stassen maintains that "because faith-loyalties are so important, they deserve a separate category for themselves."[29] There is a need to maintain the distinction "…between faith as personal trust and belief as doctrinal affirmation."[30] Faith-loyalties can either be consistent with Ground of Meaning beliefs, or in conflict. Moreover, analysis and evaluation of the ethical decision making process may at times omit, or overemphasize the importance of how faith-loyalties relate to the Ground of Meaning.

The proposed evaluative model would necessarily be required to draw lines of connection between the interpretation of Jude's Ground of Meaning and the faith-loyalties demonstrated in the letter. Is "faith" in the Epistle of Jude seen as objective or subjective? Is it something one does, or something one affirms? The faith-loyalties variable, and its interconnectedness to Ground of Meaning is vital for a proper understanding of how Jude's ethic has been interpreted, and how it should be interpreted. Conclusions about the faith-loyalties dimension should be logically connected to an interpretation's conclusions regarding Jude's particular worldview. If not, the evaluative model should facilitate the identification of inconsistencies within a specific scholarly approach to the study of the Epistle of Jude.

Group Loyalties. This variable concerns itself with how "people are powerfully influenced by loyalties to family, to friends, to the place where they work, to race and nation and interest-group ideology."[31] The issues of social location, group dynamics, relationship to authority, and many other sociological categories are the force behind this variable. Identification of group loyalties and interests helps to demonstrate the consistency or inconsistency with ground of meaning beliefs. In addition, it may help to clarify the significance behind the mode of moral discourse, or explain the threat perception that dominates a perceived situation.

Ultimate Center of Value and Loyalty. The final variable in the loyalties, interests, trust quadrant is the identification of the ultimate center of value. This variable is the heart of ethical decision making. It is what an individual or group argues for in reaction to a perceived situation, out of response to a specific ground of meaning, and with reference to a particular mode of moral discourse. Stassen cites the words of Ralph Potter who argues that the center of value is:

the fixed point, the hub, the central concern, the starting point, in relation to which, and even for the sake of which authors are inclined to select and marshal their facts and theories.[32]

The proposed evaluative model must identify how Jude's center of value has been identified and interpreted by previous scholarship. It must determine whether the identification and interpretation are consistent with conclusions about ground of meaning, mode of moral discourse, and the perception of the situation.

A Model for Evaluating the Interpretation
of Jude's Ethical Admonitions

Criteria for evaluation of ethical admonition and ethical argument in biblical texts have not been readily available. The critical variables in evaluating Christian social ethics, established by Potter and refined by Stassen, provide a sound foundation for the creation of a model designed to evaluate how the ethical arguments and admonitions of biblical texts have been previously interpreted.[33] The variables are not arbitrary, they stem from recognized scholarship, and most importantly, they offer insight into the processes that drive ethical admonition.

The proposed evaluative model will only alter the content of the variables. The major strength of Stassen's model is its ability to identify the relationships between the various dimensions and variables; therefore, the basic structure of the model will be retained. The basic content of each variable will follow Stassen's model. For the purposes of the proposed model, however, the variables will be established with particular concern for analysis of how the Epistle of Jude has been interpreted.

Jude's Mode of Moral Discourse

The first quadrant in the proposed model focuses on evaluation of how Jude's style of reasoning, or mode of moral discourse has been interpreted.

Jude's Mode of Moral Discourse

The Characterization of Jude's Argument
Is Jude understood as a...
Situationist?
Legalist?
Principlist?
Contextualist?

Fig. 6

Following Stassen's schematic, the proposed model requires analysis of how scholarship has interpreted the presentation of Jude's argument. Blunt characterizations of Jude as "mere denunciation," violent polemic, pesher exegesis, or supreme rhetoric need to be classified according to the criteria established in the model. Analysis at this level would determine if a particular scholar understands Jude to be operating at the particular judgment level, the moral rules level, the principles level, or at the level of basic beliefs. Moreover, if, for example, a particular scholar characterizes Jude as a "legalist" or as operating at the moral rules level, does such a characterization logically proceed from the evidence of the letter, or from other conclusions reached about the ground of meaning, the perception of the situation, and loyalties, interests, and trusts. The proposed evaluative model establishes the following critical variables for evaluating Jude's mode of moral discourse.

Jude's Ground of Meaning

In Stassen's description of the critical variables involved with ethical decision making, the determination about ground of meaning is essential to a proper understanding of how the processes of ethical argument occur. In like manner, the importance of establishing how Jude's ground of meaning has been interpreted is essential for evaluation of how Jude's ethical admonitions have been interpreted. Ground of meaning conclusions influence mode of moral discourse, perception of the situation, and to some extent loyalties, interests, and trust. Stated conclusions about the nature of these critical variables, must be logically connected to where ground of meaning has been located by a particular scholar.

Jude's Ground of Meaning

Apocalyptic Worldview
Ecclesiastical (Early Catholic) Worldview

Fig. 7

For evaluation of Jude's ground of meaning, the proposed model limits the possibilities to two primary categories: (1) an apocalyptic worldview, and (2) an "early Catholic" or ecclesiastical worldview. This limitation is based on the fact that the debate about the character of the Epistle of Jude has revolved primarily around the poles of Jude as an "early catholic" letter, or as a Jewish-Christian letter saturated with apocalyptic imagery. While it must be acknowledged that there are other possible locations for Jude's ground of meaning, these two principle classifications offer the best possibility for evaluation of previous interpretations.

Jude's Perception of the Situation

How Jude's perception of the situation has been interpreted centers on the issues of perceived threat, and the nature, degree, and linkage of that threat. As chapter one demonstrates, most interpretations of Jude and 2 Peter rely on

---

Jude's Perception of the Situation

The Nature of the Threat: Behavior? Teaching?
The Degree of the Threat: Specific heresy?
(e.g., Gnosticism, Antinomianism)
Linkage: To Pauline Thought? To 2 Peter?
Authority: Pseudepigraphy?

Fig. 8

establishing a specific "heretical" threat, and then building the remainder of the interpretation around that threat. The proposed model must be able to identify how the "threat" in Jude has been interpreted. First, the model will identify how the interpretation classifies the nature of the threat. Is it false teaching, or simply immoral behavior? Is it a general threat to all Christians, or a more specific concern about a particular group. Second, concerning degree, and linkage, the model would, for example, discriminate between interpretations that understand the threat as a well-developed heresy stemming from misunderstood Pauline theology, and those interpretations that emphasize the libertine behavior and see no evidence of a particular false doctrine.

The perception of the situation dimension also evaluates how the issue of authority in the Epistle of Jude has been interpreted. The question of pseudepigraphical authorship, apostolic authority, the locus, legitimacy, and limits of Jude's authority are all essential for this critical variable.

Jude's Loyalties, Interests, and Trusts

The final quadrant in the proposed evaluative model will deal with how Jude's loyalties, interests, and trusts have been interpreted. It deals primarily with the question of how scholars have understood "faith" in the Epistle of Jude, but the variable is also concerned with how Jude's group loyalties have

---

Jude's Loyalties, Interests, and Trusts

The Faith Dimension: How is "faith" understood in Jude?
Group Loyalties
Ultimate Center of Value and Loyalty: doctrine? authority? correct behavior?

Fig. 9

been interpreted. Moreover, the model will seek to identify where scholars have located the ultimate center of value and loyalty in the Epistle of Jude (e.g., doctrine, correct behavior, church authority, etc.).

The four quadrants of the proposed model relate to each other along the same lines as the four dimensions in Stassen's model. Following Stassen's presentation, the model can be illustrated as follows:

**A Model for Evaluating the Interpretation
of Jude's Ethical Admonitions**

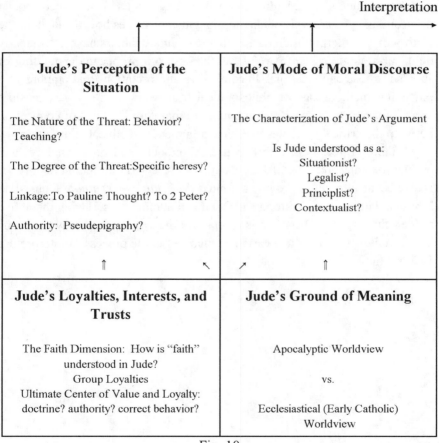

Interpretation

Jude's Perception of the Situation	Jude's Mode of Moral Discourse
The Nature of the Threat: Behavior? Teaching? The Degree of the Threat:Specific heresy? Linkage:To Pauline Thought? To 2 Peter? Authority: Pseudepigraphy?	The Characterization of Jude's Argument Is Jude understood as a: Situationist? Legalist? Principlist? Contextualist?
Jude's Loyalties, Interests, and Trusts	**Jude's Ground of Meaning**
The Faith Dimension: How is "faith" understood in Jude? Group Loyalties Ultimate Center of Value and Loyalty: doctrine? authority? correct behavior?	Apocalyptic Worldview vs. Ecclesiastical (Early Catholic) Worldview

Fig. 10

It is hoped that the ability of Stassen's model to identify and critique the logical relationships between critical variables will translate to the proposed model for evaluating the interpretation of Jude's ethical admonitions. If so, the evaluative model should point to both the strengths and weaknesses of previous interpretations, and offer some insight into how Jude's ethical argument and ethical admonitions ought to be interpreted.

The importance of the integrative strength of the evaluative model cannot be overemphasized. This analysis argues from the premise that previous scholarship in its analysis of the Epistle of Jude has emphasized particular critical variables to the detriment of a more integrative approach that seeks to understand Jude's ethical admonition stemming from an established ground of meaning. The analysis of chapter three demonstrates how throughout the history of the interpretation of the Epistle of Jude scholars have consistently held out a single critical variable as the key to a proper understanding of Jude's purpose and message. In contrast to interpretations that emphasize a particular methodology or philosophical framework, this study suggests a more integrative approach that attempts to maintain the lines of connection between the critical variables in ethical argument and ethical admonition.

Chapter three is an effort to use the model to identify, analyze, and evaluate the interpretation of Jude's ethic as presented throughout history. It is in effect an attempt to provide a limited *Forschungsgeschichte* focused on how scholars have understood Jude's ethical admonitions. Using the above model, an effort has been made to classify the various scholarly positions based on the essential critical variables involved in the process of interpreting Jude's ethic.

Chapter Three

An Evaluation of the Interpretation
of Jude's Ethical Admonition

The order of analysis will proceed from a brief examination of the limited interpretation of Jude offered by the early church, to the views articulated during the period of the Reformation by Erasmus, Luther, and Calvin, and finally to the scholarship of the nineteenth and twentieth centuries. More emphasis is placed on recent twentieth century interpretations because the discriminating power of the evaluative model is emphasized in the more diverse interpretations of more recent years. The analysis itself will offer a brief summary, evaluation, and list of strengths and weaknesses for each interpretation examined.

Early Church Interpretations

Actual comment on the Epistle of Jude is extremely limited in the writings of the early church. For the most part Jude's presence is limited to proof text in the debate concerning canonicity, either for or against Jude, and the use of apocryphal writings. There are, however, a few instances where writers in the early church offered significant comment. The letter is cited or alluded to by Clement of Alexandria (*The Instructor* 2:1, 3:8; *The Stromata* 3:2, 6:8; and *Fragments on the Epistle of Jude*); Origen (*Commentary on Matthew* 10:17:5); Hippolytus (*A Discourse* 10); and Tertullian (*On the Apparel of Women* 1:3; *To His Wife* 2:2; *On Modesty* 18). The limited scope of the commentary does not allow a full analysis based on the evaluative model, but a few conclusions can be drawn.

When the early church thinkers did offer comment on Jude, the interpretation centered on the moral rules level. Despite Origen's assessment that the letter is "of few lines…but filled with the beautiful words of heavenly grace" (*Commentary on Matthew* 10:17:5), most early interpretations of the letter see Jude as a legalist.[1] In the late second century, Clement of Alexandria offers a significant commentary on the text of Jude itself.[2] Clement identifies Jude as a "catholic" letter, written by Jude "…the brother of the sons of Joseph." Clement's "legalist" interpretation of Jude is seen clearly in his comments on verse 5: "…that is, that He might train them through punishment." Clement's emphasis on punishment as a means of instruction is also seen in *The Instructor* 3:8 where he again cites Jude 5 and comments: "By guarding against sinning, we guard against suffering .... For punishments and threats are for this end, that fearing the penalty we may abstain from sinning." Clement does not entirely miss the pastoral concern of Jude—he cites Jude 22–23 in his description of a faithful and compassionate person (*Strom.* 6:8)—but Jude's primary concern as understood by Clement is to prophetically refute the heresy of Carpocratian Gnosticism (*Strom.* 3:2).

While it is acknowledged that the proposed categories cannot be forced on ancient writing, it does seem that Clement can be classified as understanding Jude to be a legalist who perceived a heretical threat of some degree, and argued from a moral rules level that held out punishment as a deterrent to breaking the rules. The weakness of this interpretation falls fundamentally in its inattention to Jude's ground of meaning, and how that ground of meaning relates to the mode of discourse and the perception of the situation (a circumstance that flaws much modern scholarship).

In the Nicene and Post-Nicene period, The Epistle of Jude is again primarily relegated to proof text in the debate surrounding the ecclesiastical canon. In *City of God* Augustine cites Jude in his argument against the writings of Enoch:

> What of Enoch, the seventh from Adam? Does not the canonical epistle of
> the Apostle Jude declare that he prophesied? But the writings of these men
> could not be held as authoritative either among the Jews or us, on account of
> their too great antiquity, which made it seem needful to regard them with
> suspicion, lest false things should be set forth instead of true (18:38).[3]

Augustine also notes the polemical emphasis in the Epistle of the Epistle of Jude citing v. 19: "that they who have separated from the Church have not this Spirit, the Apostle Jude has declared most plainly, saying 'Who separate themselves, natural, having not the Spirit'" (*Sermons on New-Testament Lessons* 21:30).[4] Again, while there is not a direct characterization of Jude's ethical admonitions, some tentative evaluations can be offered. Augustine's identification of Jude as "an apostle" suggests an understanding of Jude as authoritative, and worthy of loyalty. Augustine clearly places Jude within the ecclesiastical worldview, arguing against "those who have separated from the church."

The evidence from this period is so meager as to virtually eliminate it from our consideration by the evaluative model; however, it is clear that the value of the letter during the early centuries of the church was primarily one of support for positions on canon, and against various heretical positions that were a threat to the church. The beginning of Jude's entrenchment in the ecclesiastical or "early Catholic" worldview was initiated during these centuries, and would come to full fruition during the period of the Reformation.

The Period of the Reformation

Writing between 1519 and 1521, Erasmus states that "Jude rages at some length against those who, blinded by their own desires, were opposing the gospel" (*The Argument of the Epistle of Jude*).[5] Erasmus' interpretation of Jude is characterized by three primary assertions. First, Erasmus' interpretation focuses more on the ethical implications of Jude's argument. While Erasmus betrays the expected ecclesiastical view of "the faith," which he characterizes with terms like "purity" and "foundation," the danger to the faith is depicted in terms of ungodly behavior as over against heresy, or false teaching:

> Though we have delivered the doctrine of the gospel to you honestly and purely just as we received it from Christ, nevertheless certain ungodly persons have unobtrusively entered your midst under the disguise of religion and have crept like wolves into the Lord's sheepfold. Their appearance of godliness commends them, though they are the enemies of genuine godliness (*Paraphrase on the Epistle of Jude*).[6]

For Erasmus, the clear distinction depicted in the Epistle of Jude is between the godly lives of the addressees, and the ungodly behavior of the troublemakers. Jude writes against "…men who, while you are living pure and chaste lives and are espousing evangelical love, are present, disfiguring your flock like blemishes…they indulge themselves privately in extravagant carousing (*Para. Ep. Jude*)."[7] The nature of the threat as presented by Erasmus is clearly the problem of immoral behavior.

Erasmus' second assertion deals with Jude's perception of the situation and the linkage variable. Erasmus clearly links the threat in Jude to problems predicted by Paul and Peter. Erasmus asserts that Jude argues:

> This opposition should not, however, be thought to be something novel because the opponents were destined long ago for this end and it was predicted by the apostles that people of this sort would creep into the Christian flock (*Arg. Ep. Jude*).[8]

Erasmus' link to Peter and Paul is more explicit in *Para. Ep. Jude*: "Their malice will cause you less distress, dearly beloved, if you remember that the other apostles of our Lord Jesus Christ predicted this…in particular Paul and Peter."[9] This degree of linkage is significant in that Erasmus draws direct lines of connection between Jude's apostolic authority and the apostolic authority of Peter and Paul.

Erasmus' third assertion about the nature of the argument in the Epistle of Jude is his interpretation of the twofold thrust of Jude's admonitions. Erasmus identifies two distinct elements in Jude's argument:

> He arms his readers against them by urging them to be ready either to restrain these men through reprimands or to save them through admonitions. But if his readers are unable to accomplish this, they are at least to get themselves ready for the coming of Christ (*Arg. Ep. Jude*).[10]

Erasmus sees in the Epistle of Jude the admonition to "save everyone" (*Para. Ep. Jude* v. 22), and an understanding of mercy that incorporates all individuals:

> It is fitting to heal the errors of others all the more mercifully because no one who dwells in this wretched body can avoid being stained, for that is simply not within human power (*Para. Ep. Jude* vv. 22–23).[11]

Erasmus' interpretation of the Epistle of Jude recognizes the importance of mercy, and the significance of members of the community preparing for the "coming of Christ."

While Erasmus' treatment of the Epistle of Jude still places Jude's ground of meaning firmly within the ecclesiastical worldview, there are elements of the interpretation that are distinct. The nature of the threat is clearly related to bad behavior rather than incorrect teaching. While "faith" is understood primarily as doctrine, Erasmus apparently understands Jude's ultimate center of value to be located in proper behavior between members of the Christian community.

The characterization of Jude as "raging" against the opponents bespeaks a characterization of Jude arguing from a particular judgment level. Yet, Erasmus' emphasis on Jude's concern for ethics, and the remedies that he identifies in the text suggests that his interpretation might be classified more correctly as emphasizing principles, or basic beliefs. Again, the critical variables do not precisely fit the context of Erasmus' approach to the letter. They do point, however, to the elements of Jude's argument that he emphasizes: an ecclesiastical or "early Catholic" worldview, perceiving of a behavioral threat, linked to the teachings of Paul and Peter, which understands the ultimate value to be proper relationship between individuals in the church, and applies the principles of mercy and preparedness to the context of the situation.

A strength of Erasmus' approach to the Epistle of Jude is that it lifts Jude's mode of ethical argument from the particular judgment level (e.g., mere denunciation, or polemic) to the principles level where principles are applied to a particular context. The weakness, as with most older treatments, is that not enough is said about how Jude's mode of moral discourse relates to his ground of meaning.

Writing at about the same time as Erasmus, Martin Luther expresses strong and influential opinions about the nature and value of the Epistle of Jude. Luther attributes the letter to the apostle Judas in Mark 6:3; however, he believes that "…this letter does not seem to have been written by the real apostle, for in it Jude refers to himself as a much later disciple of the apostles."[12] In addition, Luther sees in Jude nothing "…special beyond pointing to the Second Epistle of Saint Peter, from which it has borrowed nearly all the words."[13] Luther recognizes that Jude's use of non-canonical writings has caused it to be rejected by some of the church fathers, but says "…this is not sufficient reason for rejecting a book."[14] Luther's ultimate assessment of the Epistle of Jude, however, removes it from consideration by those seeking the foundations of the faith:

Therefore, although I value this book, it is an epistle that need not be counted among the chief books which are supposed to lay the foundations of faith.[15]

Heiligenthal argues that this negative assessment of the value of the letter has given Jude a *Schattendasein* among subsequent scholarship.[16]

In his interpretation of the Epistle of Jude, Luther seeks to draw significant parallels to his own situation. He suggests that the letter "…is nothing more than an epistle directed against our clerics—bishops, priests, and monks."[17] The opponents, or troublemakers are identified as "…preachers who are introducing another teaching alongside the faith."[18] Luther identifies this added element as the false teaching of salvation by works:

> But they deny the Lord Christ with deeds and with works. They regard themselves, not Him, as their Lord. When they proclaim that fasting, pilgrimages, founding churches, chastity, obedience, poverty, etc., are the way to salvation, they direct people to their works and keep silence about Christ. This is tantamount to saying: 'Christ is of no use to you; His works do not help you. But you must merit salvation with your own works.'[19]

Luther links this problem to a misunderstanding of Paul's preaching, and compares Paul's problem in Galatians with the problem faced by Jude, namely "…that in many people he [Satan] transforms the freedom for which Christ has set us free into an opportunity for the flesh."[20]

Luther's understanding of Jude's perception of the situation emphasizes false teaching that allows incorrect behavior. In Luther's context, the specific heresy can be described as salvation by works, and it is clearly linked to similar problems faced by the apostle Paul. Luther's conclusions about Jude's perception of the situation stem primarily from the context of Luther's own contemporary situation, rather than from any speculation about Jude's ground of meaning.

For Luther, Jude's ultimate center of value is the understanding of "faith" alone being necessary for salvation; however, this characterization of "faith" in the Epistle of Jude is more representative of Luther's ultimate center of value. Jude's reference to "faith" (vv. 3 and 20) becomes for Luther an opportunity to delineate the Christian way of life:

> Faith is the foundation on which one should build. But to build up means to

increase from day to day in the knowledge of God and Jesus Christ. This is done through the Holy Spirit. Now when we are built up in this way, we should not do a single work in order to merit anything by it or to be saved; but everything must be done for the benefit of our neighbor.[21]

In Luther's interpretation of the Epistle of Jude, primary emphasis is placed on determining the perception of the situation, and on a proper delineation of the faith dimension. There is very little attention given to Jude's mode of moral discourse, beyond characterizing it as a letter written against the clergy. Luther's fatal flaw is that he relates most of his conclusions about the perception of the situation, and the faith dimension to his own particular situation. Rather than seeking to establish Jude's ground of meaning, Luther works out of his ground of meaning and projects his basic beliefs and concerns onto Jude's argument. Given this presuppositional mindset, it is not surprising that Luther understands Jude to be writing against the ecclesiastical abuses of Luther's own context.

John Calvin wrote his *Commentaries on the Catholic Epistles* in 1551.[22] Like Luther, Calvin's own situation bleeds through his interpretation of the Epistle of Jude. Calvin asserts that Jude's primary purpose was to write against individuals who "...under the name of Christians, had crept in, whose chief object was to lead the unstable and weak to a profane contempt of God."[23] That these types of people have always "assailed" the church is foundational for Calvin, and he characterizes Jude's argument against them in harsh terms:

He exhorts them carefully to beware of such pests. And to render them more hateful and detestable, he denounces on them the approaching vengeance of God, such as their impiety deserved.[24]

Here Calvin comes close to maintaining for Jude a mode of moral discourse which emphasizes a particular judgment, a characterization which offers no proof, which simply denounces. The suggestion that Jude identifies the opponents as "hateful" or "detestable" anticipates the characterization of Jude as "mere denunciation" which dominates much of modern scholarship.

For Calvin, the distinctions drawn by Jude are between the elect and the wicked, and the certain punishment of the later group is interpreted as motivation for the former: "But the vengeance suspended over the wicked ought to keep the elect in fear and watchfulness."[25] This understanding of punishment being held out as an instructional or motivational tool resonates with the legalist interpretation of Clement. The transgression of the troublemakers is linked to Jude's ecclesiastical worldview: "...they separated from the Church, because they would not bear the yoke of discipline, as they who indulge the flesh dislike spiritual life."[26] With Calvin, the stamp of Jude's ecclesiastical worldview becomes more pronounced. Calvin's distinctions between the elect and the wicked are superimposed on Jude's delineation of problems facing the early church and his harsh characterization of Jude's mode of argument prefigures the assessments of later scholars. Again, as with Luther, Calvin's own interests and loyalties have a significant impact on his interpretation of the ethical admonition in the Epistle of Jude.

While not all the critical variables in the evaluative model fit the preceding interpretations, some summary conclusions can be drawn about how Jude's ethical admonitions and argument were understood during the period of the Reformation. First, Jude's mode of moral discourse was characterized primarily as a particular judgment. Despite Erasmus' more positive evaluation of Jude working at the principles level, the predominant and lasting view of the reformers understood Jude to be offering harsh denunciation of troublemakers, with little or no positive message. Second, this judgment during the Reformation period left the Epistle of Jude a letter outside the canon within the canon. Third, the interpretation of Jude remained firmly linked to the ecclesiastical or "early Catholic" worldview. The interpretation of the problems faced by Jude continued to be linked to digressions from the established "faith" of the church, whether those were doctrinal, behavioral, or a combination of both. Finally, the treatments of both Luther and Calvin demonstrate the tendency of scholars to allow their own loyalties, interests, and trusts to have an impact on their interpretation of the biblical text. The full import of this tendency comes to bear in the scholarly treatment of the Epistle of Jude in the nineteenth and early twentieth centuries.

Nineteenth and Early Twentieth Century Interpretations

Robert M. Grant argues that "one of the most striking features of the development of biblical interpretation during the nineteenth century was the way in which philosophical presuppositions implicitly guided it."[27] Rationalism, skepticism, and Hegelian distinctions were the order of the day for biblical interpretation. These forces did not leave untouched the interpretation of the Epistle of Jude.

Adolf Jülicher places the responsibility for any doubts about the genuineness of the Epistle of Jude squarely on the German skepticism best represented by Friedrich Schleiermacher.[28] Jude's "second class status," established during the period of the Reformation, became firmly entrenched during the nineteenth century. Additional philosophical presuppositions would affect how the Epistle of Jude was interpreted by nineteenth century scholarship.

Working from the presumption of a Hegelian dialectic, F. C. Baur and his Tübingen followers related their conclusions about the Epistle of Jude to the letter's relationship with Paul. Heiligenthal argues that no matter how difficult or complex the issue, Baur sought to answer every question about the theological and historical background of the New Testament books by relating it to the simple contrast between Jewish and Greek Christians.[29] In particular this meant for Jude a relationship to the Pauline situation. Heiligenthal argues that in the history of interpretation, there has always been a tendency to see Jude in relation to Paul. The Tübingen School saw in Jude a late testimony against Pauline Christianity.[30]

In terms of the evaluative model, this tendency to relate the message of the Epistle of Jude to Pauline Christianity demonstrates nineteenth century scholarship's emphasis on determining Jude's perception of the situation. Of paramount importance was the determination of how Jude fit into the broader philosophical framework.[31] Jude is identified as a Jewish-Christian reaction to either Pauline theology, or some heretical position that grows out of a misunderstanding of Pauline theology.

Thus, for example, Otto Pfleiderer, *Primitive Christianity*, argues for a specific identification of the situation faced by Jude, and builds his interpretation of the entire letter around that presumption. Pfleiderer grasps at the "gnostic" characteristics found in Jude's description of the troublemakers: "...they did not recognize the Creator-God of the Old Testament as the true God of the Christians, but degraded Him to a demonic Demiurge," (v. 4); they deny the incarnation; and their immorality is linked to their Gnosticism, "...that it was held by them to be justified by it, and in a sense to be proof of their state of grace and possession of the Spirit," (v.4).[32] These "gnostic" characteristics are then linked by Pfleiderer to "…the Gnostic sect of the Carpocratians, which about 140 A.D., was founded by the Alexandrian Carpocrates and Epiphanes (father and son)."[33]

Pfleiderer's identification of the troublemakers fills out his interpretation of Jude's perception of the situation. The nature of the threat is doctrinal—a specific heresy related to a misunderstanding of grace. The degree of the threat is severe—the opponents are identified as full-blown gnostics. The threat is linked to a specific origin and place—Alexandria, and the sect of the Carpocratians. Every other aspect of Pfleiderer's interpretation hinges on how he understands Jude's perception of the situation.

Because of the specific nature of the heresy, the letter "…can scarcely have been written before the middle of the second century."[34] Moreover, the author, who was most likely an Alexandrian Hellenist, must have sought to gain authority by writing by writing under an assumed name.[35] In addition, because of the nature of the problem "there could, of course, be no question of a theoretical refutation of extravagances such as these…[Jude] contents himself with vigorous threatenings of the Divine judgment."[36] Pfleiderer's conclusion about Jude's perception of the situation colors his determination about Jude's mode of moral discourse. The author of the letter operates at the particular judgment level, expressing a severe judgment without offering supporting argument.

Perhaps most significantly, Pfleiderer's emphasis on Jude's perception of the situation requires that in the analysis of Jude's loyalties, interests, and trusts, "faith" must be understood to refer to a body of doctrine which stands in need of defence against a specific heresy. Jude's ultimate center of value and loyalty becomes for Pfleiderer a defense of the "faith once for all delivered to the saints." For Pfleiderer then, Jude's ethical admonitions are primarily related to the interpretation of the author's perception of the situation that is in turn related to the mode of moral discourse, and nature of "faith" as the ultimate center of value.

While Pfleiderer stands as a glaring example of an interpretation of Jude's ethical argument based primarily on conclusions about the perception of the situation, no less a figure than Adolf Harnack can be critiqued at the same level. Harnack, working from essentially the same philosophical and interpretive framework as Pfleiderer and the Tübingen scholars, determined that the Epistle of Jude was intended to combat Syrian gnostics.[37] Again, a determination of how Jude perceives the situation drives the whole of the interpretation. While the results of such historical investigations are often intriguing, their usefulness in understanding the ethical argument of the text is limited. Attempts to relate Jude's ethical admonitions strictly to the author's perception of the situation turn the question on its head. The evaluative model suggests that interpretation of ethical argument and admonition must grow out of an understanding of the author's ground of meaning beliefs that leads to an evaluation of the mode of moral discourse, the perception of the situation, and loyalties, interests, and trusts.

Despite the speculative nature of historical-critical studies of the Epistle of Jude, scholars continued efforts to establish the "situation" to which Jude was written. In a classic turn of the century study, J. B. Mayor produced a comprehensive study of both Jude and 2 Peter.[38] While Mayor takes a respectfully tentative approach to the critical issues surrounding the Epistle of Jude, he still rests his interpretation of Jude primarily on how he understands Jude's perception of the situation.[39] For Mayor, the nature of the threat facing Jude is "…a misgrowth of St. Paul's teaching in regard to a Salvation of free grace, 'not of words, lest any man should boast.'"[40] Jude is thoroughly familiar with "Pauline" language, and Mayor holds that even Jude's understanding of "…a Christian tradition is familiar to St. Paul, and that there are other examples in the NT of the objective use of πίστις."[41] For Mayor, Jude's perception of the situation is linked substantially to the writings and teachings of Paul.

Mayor also links Jude response to the problem to other NT writings. He draws significant comparisons, not surprisingly to James and 2 Peter, and the distinctions in the character of the three letters. Betraying a more positive view of the Epistle of James, Mayor reveals an evaluation of Jude as offering a particular judgment:

> [James]…is full of instruction for the present time, the bulk of [Jude] is made
> up of denunciations which have very much lost their force. To a modern
> reader it is curious rather than edifying.[42]

As earlier scholars had done, Mayor establishes Jude's mode of moral discourse as particular judgment based not on a sound assessment of Jude's ground of meaning beliefs, but rather on a determination of the nature, degree, and linkage of the threat situation faced by the author of Jude. Again, the elements of Jude's ethical argument and admonition are allowed to spring forth from judgments about the author's perception of the situation, rather than from some determination of the ground of meaning beliefs that are the foundation of ethical argument.

The tendency to evaluate Jude's message and worth by relying primarily on a speculative determination of Jude's perception of the situation continued to dominate scholarship in the early part of this century. Adolf Jülicher (1904) determined the problem faced by Jude was gnosticism, and argued "...whether we see in them Carpocratisis or Archontics, or members of some school that afterwards disappeared, we cannot date either them or the Epistle [of Jude] before the time of the Pastoral Epistles."[43] For Jülicher, the Epistles of Jude and 2 Peter were written to a "truly 'catholic' audience," and "...concern the Church in general; they lack the personal stamp, and necessities universally felt are met by them with counsel universal in tone."[44] Again, Jülicher approaches the letter by determining Jude's perception of the situation (gnosticism), establishes a ground of meaning (an early Catholic response), and completes his interpretation based on these criteria.

In 1901 Charles Bigg, *The Epistles of St. Peter and St. Jude*, also characterized Jude's mode of moral reasoning as particular judgment.[45] For Bigg "the style and tone of the Epistle set before us a stern and unbending nature."[46] Bigg establishes a significant link with "Pauline" thought, yet like Mayor seeks to maintain links with the "Petrine" letters. Bigg postulates two possibilities: "We must suppose either that a Petrine Epistle was recast by a friend of St. Paul's, or that a Pauline Epistle was adapted by a disciple of St. Peter's."[47] Bigg finds the former possibility the "easier of the two alternatives," and argues that Jude's perception of the situation understands the threat to be in the form of "Antinomian movements, which had themselves no principle except a gross misconception of Pauline freedom."[48]

The understanding of the perception of the situation which links the problem faced in Jude with "Pauline" theology betrays the influence of the Tübingen philosophy on Bigg. Also, Bigg's desire to maintain apostolic authority for 2 Peter, requires that he place Jude within a situation where both Paul and Peter play a significant role. Bigg argues for the priority of 2 Peter and postulates a scenario where Peter took alarm at the behavioral excesses in

Corinth and wrote 2 Peter. Jude received a copy of this letter and wrote a circular letter to his churches. For Bigg, this description of the situation in the Epistle of Jude provides "a perfectly natural explanation of Jude 3" and allows him to maintain genuine apostolic authority for 2 Peter. Bigg's emphasis on the perception of the situation in Jude focuses on the threat which is linked to Paul and to Peter. In addition, it understands the nature of authority in both Jude and 2 Peter to be genuine and not assumed.

Bigg's emphasis on the perception of the situation affects his interpretation of Jude's mode of moral discourse. The strong link to both Paul and Peter drives Bigg's understanding of how Jude makes his argument. Bigg states that "compared with 2 Peter he [Jude] exhibits a certain hastiness and tendency to take things at their worst…on the other hand, Jude is in closer intellectual sympathy with St. Paul."[49] Bigg's emphasis on Jude's perception of the situation, and his devotion to a particular philosophical framework (the priority of 2 Peter) is not unexpected and in fact demonstrates the remarkable consistency of scholarship that dominated the late nineteenth and early twentieth centuries. The approaches of F. H. Chase,[50] Theodor Zahn,[51] James Moffatt,[52] J. W. C. Wand[53] all maintain a level of commitment to understanding Jude's perception of the situation. In addition, their own particular loyalties, interests, and trusts have significant influence on their respective conclusions about the nature and purpose of the Epistle of Jude.

The historical-critical method and the particular philosophical frameworks that came to influence how historical data was interpreted continued to dominate the scholarly approach to the New Testament during the middle part of the twentieth century. In addition, the particular study of Jude and 2 Peter became highly derivative. Analysis of the Epistle of Jude during this period is limited almost exclusively to minor treatments in several commentary series where previous approaches to the interpretation of the letter are reiterated with little critical analysis.[54]

Recent Twentieth Century Interpretations

With the advent of diverse methodological approaches to New Testament study and the increasing availability of significant background sources, recent studies of the Epistle of Jude demonstrate a variety of interpretive expressions. While most treatments are still limited to commentaries within a series and are often linked with interpretation of 2 Peter or James, there is a renewed interest in individual studies of the Epistle of Jude demonstrated by the increasing number of commentaries, articles, and monographs devoted to the interpretation of this letter.[55]

The last section of this chapter devotes itself to an analysis of several significant contributions to the study of the Epistle of Jude beginning in the early seventies and moving through the next two decades. Because of the variety of methodologically driven approaches to the study of the New Testament which by their very nature emphasize particular critical variables to the detriment of others, the discriminating power of the evaluative model is more pronounced. The evaluative model will allow an analysis of those approaches which have emphasized Jude's mode of moral discourse, Jude's perception of the situation, Jude's loyalties, interests and trusts, and finally those few interpretations which have sought a foundation in the identification of Jude's ground of meaning beliefs.

Jude and the Mode of Moral Discourse

In 1978 E. Earle Ellis opened a new door on the interpretation of the Epistle of Jude. Ellis' "Prophecy and Hermeneutic in Jude" convincingly argued for a new understanding of the way in which the author of Jude formulates the argument against the opponents.[56] Ellis sees in the letter "'commentary', (i.e., 'midrash') patterns common to first century Judaism."[57] Citing the shift of tense that marks each commentary section, and the use of the "quasi-formulaic" οὗτος and οὗτός ἐστιν, Ellis suggests a commentary pattern where OT or extrabiblical citations are applied to present problems within the believing community. Ellis confirms his conclusion about the commentary pattern by citing "the extraordinarily abundant catchword connections...which are the hall-mark of the midrashic procedure."[58]

Ellis' remarkable treatment of the central section of the Epistle of Jude forces scholars to recognize that "the whole piece (5–19) is a carefully worked-out commentary."[59] This is the overriding strength of Ellis' interpretation. Yet, it is also the most glaring weakness.

Ellis' assertion that the central section (vv.5–19) is a carefully crafted commentary which "Jude has then introduced (1–4) and supplied with a concluding exhortation (20–23)" does not take cognizance of the unity of the letter and the importance of the opening and closing appeals (vv. 3–4, 20–23) and the doxology (vv. 24–25). The emphasis on the central section leads Ellis to conclude that "Jude's writing, then is a midrash on the theme of judgment for which the letter-form provides a convenient dress."[60]

Certainly the central section of the letter focuses on the theme of judgment, but the introduction and conclusion should not be relegated to mere addenda to the more unified central section. On the contrary, the important information found in these few verses helps to establish an important aspect of Jude's ground of meaning. Ellis' approach establishes a single thrust for Jude's ethical admonition, namely God's judgment on those who are characterized in verses 5–19.

Ellis' emphasis on Jude as a careful piece of exegetical commentary places his interpretation under the category of mode of moral discourse. The argument that Jude applies OT and extrabiblical texts to a current problem within the community suggests that Ellis understands Jude to be principlist, or perhaps a contextualist. For Ellis, Jude argues from a set of established principles, or basic beliefs in response to a new situation. The articulation of Jude's commentary method removes the particular judgment characterization of the letter which was so prevalent in late nineteenth and early twentieth century scholarship. The rest of Ellis' interpretation is directly related to his description of Jude's mode of moral reasoning.

Concerning Jude's perception of the situation, Ellis suggests strong links to Paul and the problem facing the church in Acts 15. The emphasis on Jude's mode of reasoning as careful commentary allows Ellis to argue for a specific identification of the author (the Jude of Acts 15) and situation (the false teaching opposed in the Jerusalem decree).[61] In addition, Ellis holds that the very way in which the letter is constructed reveals "something of the praxis of the early Christian mission and the relationship of its two major components," (Hebrews and Hellenists).[62] Ellis posits a "positive" ecumenical role for the Epistle of Jude standing between Jew and Greek, holding the two together, guarding against behavioral and doctrinal excess.

The weakness of Ellis' assertion is that the conclusion stems not from the establishment of Jude's ground of meaning beliefs, but rather from the application of Jude's mode of moral discourse to a particular situation and the subsequent extrapolation of a more general conclusion about the nature and purpose of Jude's letter. This does not diminish the significance of Ellis' approach to the letter. It does, however, point to the need to identify Jude's ground of meaning beliefs and apply them to the other critical variables which influence ethical admonition. More emphasis on the important introduction and conclusion of the letter might help to establish the important aspects of Jude's ground of meaning which can in turn be applied to the mode of moral discourse, the perception of the situation, and the loyalties, interests, and trusts revealed in the letter.

In 1988, Duane F. Watson, *Invention, Arrangement, and Style: Rhetorical Criticism of Jude and 2 Peter*, brought the significant weight of rhetorical analysis to his interpretation of Jude and 2 Peter.[63] For Watson the key to a proper understanding of the purpose and message of the Epistle of Jude lies in a proper understanding of certain rhetorical elements which he identifies in the letter. Watson's detailed rhetorical analysis of the letter leads him to conclude that "the author of Jude is skilled in the rhetoric of his time…to do justice to its content, the epistle must be interpreted in light of the conventions of Greco-Roman rhetoric.[64]

With this end in mind, the elements of Watson's argument can be summarized and evaluated. Watson sees in Jude an example of deliberative rhetoric "intended to advise and dissuade the audience with reference to a particular action."[65] Watson identifies the *Exordium* (v.3), the "Quasi-*Exordium*" (vv. 1–2) which he also calls the Epistolary Prescript, the *Narratio* (v. 4), the *Probatio* (vv. 5–16), the *Peroratio* (vv. 17–23), and the Doxology or "Quasi-*Peroratio*"(vv. 24–25).[66] Within these broad rhetorical categories, Watson also discusses the various rhetorical tools which Jude employs in carrying out the deliberative task.

Watson argues that "the bulk of Jude (vv. 4–19) is clearly of a demonstrative nature and is essentially a barbed denunciation of the sectarians based on their character and deeds."[67] Here, Watson stresses the importance of the central section of the letter which Ellis also asserts. Watson, however, recognizes the importance of verses 20–23 (the *Adfectus*) where "Jude now appeals to audience emotion to dissuade them from similar activity and to persuade them to work against the sectarians' influence in their own lives and the lives of others."[68]

Vital to Watson's argument and to our understanding of Jude's rhetorical skill are the rhetorical constraints which Watson identifies within the letter. Watson holds that these:

> Rhetorical constraints have the power to direct the decision and action
> needed to modify the exigence. These include beliefs, attitudes, documents,
> facts, traditions, images, interests, motives, and, once the rhetor adds
> discourse, the rhetor's ethos, proofs, and style. These constitute two main
> types of constraint: *those created by the rhetor and his discourse*, and *those
> inherent in the situation.*[69]

When applied to the evaluative model of critical variables, Watson's emphasis
on rhetorical constraints reveals an understanding of Jude as a principlist
whose argument flows out of principles (rhetorical constraints) to a specific
judgment ("action needed to modify the exigence").

Watson identifies both teleological and deontological constraints. The
teleological or utilitarian constraints are those that are created by the rhetor
and his discourse. Here, as in the principlist model, the means (ethos, proofs,
style, e.g., "barbed denunciation") is justified by the positive consequences of
the end (modified behavior). The deontological constraints are those which are
inherent in the situation (beliefs, attitudes, documents, facts, traditions,
images, interests, and motives, e.g., the authoritative constraints of the OT,
extra-biblical Jewish traditions, and apostolic authority) and are skillfully
employed by the rhetor in order to bring about the desired result.

The clear strength of Watson's approach is his emphasis on the unity and
clarity of Jude's mode of moral discourse. Like Ellis, Watson establishes a
clear mode of moral discourse and builds his interpretation around it. While
Ellis places Jude against the background of Jewish scriptural exegesis, Watson
argues for an interpretation of Jude in light of Greco-Roman rhetoric. In
addition, Watson maintains a positive thrust for Jude in verses 22–23 (the
Adfectus).

Two weaknesses are readily apparent. First, the evaluative model
suggests that Watson understands Jude to be a principlist who applies both
teleological and deontological constraints to the situation in order to effect a
certain outcome. While this argument is compelling, there is no attempt to
relate those constraints or principles to Jude's ground of meaning beliefs.
Second, it has been demonstrated that many rhetorical elements which have
been argued for in Jude are in fact not products of conscious creation by Jude,
but simply descriptive of the natural argumentative style of Jude.[70] Watson's
commitment to a particular methodology reveals his loyalties, interests and

trusts; it does not, however, limit Jude's mode of moral discourse to the rules and conventions of Greco-Roman rhetoric.

Recently, J. Daryl Charles, *Literary Strategy in the Epistle of Jude*, has tried to bridge the gap between the approaches of Ellis and Watson.[71] Charles seeks to "unveil a literary strategy at work" in the Epistle of Jude by identifying and understanding the function of the literary resources available to the writer.[72] While Ellis sees Jude against the backdrop of Jewish exegesis and Watson understands Greco-Roman rhetorical conventions, Charles characterizes Jude as a broad "rhetorical-theological polemic…which employs a highly stylized literary approach."[73] Where Ellis and Watson want to exclude and specify, Charles seeks to identify Jude's mode of discourse as "…apocalyptic, midrashic, liturgical, and rhetorical."[74] This eclectic approach allows Charles to focus on relationship between form and content.

Charles concludes that both form and content are vital for a proper understanding of the message of Jude. Jude demonstrates that "truth comes to…the audience, *through literary form*."[75] In order to truly understand the significance of the Epistle of Jude, the literary strategy must be identified. In Jude the literary form "reveals a literary approach…with specific, well-calculated rhetorical effects aimed at addressing *particular pastoral needs*."[76] Charles understands Jude's primary pastoral concern to be exhorting "…the *faithful* by painting in graphic terms the fate of the *unfaithful*."[77]

Like Watson, and to some extent Ellis, Charles understands Jude to be a principlist who argues from established principles for a specific ethical outcome. Again, both teleolgocial (literary-rhetorical strategies employed by Jude) and deontological strategies (Jude's location within a Palestinian milieu) are identified by Charles. A particular strength of Charles' approach is his effort to relate the form of Jude's argument (Jude's mode of moral discourse) to the content of Jude's message (Jude's ground of meaning). The weakness of Charles' approach, however, is that the identification of form precedes the identification of content. The evaluative model suggests that the mode of moral discourse must stem from ground of meaning beliefs. Charles reverses the approach by establishing a literary strategy and then extrapolating the theological content.

Each of the above interpretations emphasizes Jude's mode of moral discourse. The strength of these interpretations is their emphasis on the literary unity and purpose of the Epistle of Jude. Their emphasis on Jude's mode of moral discourse, whether identified as Jewish exegesis, Greco-Roman rhetoric, or an eclectic mix of literary strategies, demonstrates that Jude is not just "mere denunciation," or "violent polemic;" rather, the letter is a well crafted literary whole with a definite purpose and message. The weakness of these interpretations is demonstrated by the evaluative model. There is either no attempt to relate ground of meaning beliefs to the mode of moral discourse, or the attempt is made in reverse. Each of these interpretations might be strengthened by an attempt to establish Jude's ground of meaning beliefs and in turn relate those beliefs to the mode of moral discourse identified in the letter.

Jude and the Perception of the Situation

While literary approaches to the study of the Epistle of Jude emphasize the mode of moral discourse, scholars continue to press for a resolution to the question of Jude's perception of the situation. In 1971 Douglas J. Rowston, "The Setting of the Letter of Jude," tried to establish a position for the Epistle of Jude in the developing tension between eschatology and ecclesiology.[78] Rowston holds open the thesis "…that Jude, after James and before 2 Peter, was opposing a misunderstanding of Paul which had gnostic nuances."[79] This thesis is then tested by Rowston who examines five factors: (1) the nature of the heresy opposed; (2) the traditional literary materials used; (3) Jude's relationship to the apostolic age; (4) Jude's redaction of the sources; and (5) the influence of Jude on early Christianity.[80]

Rowston concludes that the heretics facing Jude were antinomian proto-gnostics who misunderstood the Pauline doctrine of justification by faith. In order to combat this heresy, the author of Jude brought together particular literary resources which betray an indebtedness to a Palestinian milieu. Consistent with the Palestinian backdrop, the pseudepigraphal author of the letter chose a pseudonym from within Palestinian dynastic Christianity. Rowston concludes the test of his thesis by praising the "homeletical effectiveness" of the letter. Rowston stresses the "strong monologue and weak dialogue" which characterizes the Epistle of Jude; yet the theological value of the letter is "dubious."[81] Rowston understands Jude to be a strong, well thought out statement produced in a time of ethical and creedal development and intended to combat antinomian behavior. For Rowston the continuing positive value of the Epistle of Jude for the Church lies in its communicative strength. Rowston argues that the Church should learn from Jude's strong monologue and weak dialogue.

Rowston's emphasis on Jude's perception of the situation allows him to develop his thesis without establishing a particular ground of meaning for the author of the letter. The nature of the threat is behavioral with overtones of doctrinal error. Rowston posits strong links to both Paul and James, and in turn 2 Peter. The threat perceived by Jude is directly linked to a misunderstanding of Paul, and the solution presented by Jude is directly linked to James and Palestinian dynastic Christianity. Faith is understood to represent a developing creed, and Jude is characterized as a situationist, whose "strong monologue" leaves no room for dialogue about the nature of that faith.

To his credit, Rowston seizes upon Jude's apocalyptic worldview as the means by which correction should occur. In this, however, Rowston fails to establish a ground of meaning for Jude. Rowston argues that "apocalypticism was the vehicle by which the author of Jude sought to circumvent the neo-Pauline antinomian proto-gnostics in his community or communities."[82] While Rowston comes close to establishing a ground of meaning for Jude within an apocalyptic worldview, the issue actually addressed is Jude's mode of moral discourse. Jude uses "strong monologue" self-consciously set within an apocalyptic worldview. Rowston's effort to make apocalyptic the means of correction displaces Jude's ground of meaning.[83]

In 1974 Walter Grundmann, *Der Brief des Judas und der zweite Brief des Petrus*, further articulated the relationship between the Jewish-Christian letter of Jude and the misunderstandings that developed out of the misappropriation of Paul's gospel as a message of freedom.[84] Grundmann emphasizes Jude's rebuke of ungodly behavior as over against false doctrine. Both Jude and 2 Peter engage their opponents not in their doctrine, but in their abuse of freedom which is displayed in their extravagant lifestyle, and in their arrogant conduct.[85] Jude and 2 Peter argue against individuals who boast of their new freedom in their "...scorn of cosmic forces, community order, and ethical binding orders."[86]

Grundmann argues that the nature of the threat facing the author of the letter of Jude is best characterized as ἀσέβια. This ungodliness threatens the church both from within and from without. The degree of the threat is severe. It threatens to cause Christians to fall away from the serious life which God requires. The threat is so serious, that the author of the letter renounces any dispute with the false teachers' doctrine, and limits the mode of moral discourse to ethical reproach.[87] While Grundmann acknowledges that some type of doctrinal error may be at the heart of the ungodly abuse of freedom, he holds that the author of Jude does not engage the opponents at the level of their doctrine, but rather at the level of their behavior.[88]

Like Rowston, Grundmann's emphasis on Jude's perception of the situation does not require reflection about the nature of Jude's ground of meaning beliefs. The strength of Grundmann's approach is his articulation of the nature of the threat faced by Jude. Grundmann's identification of the nature of the threat as ἀσέβια places any theoretical dispute about doctrine in the background, and puts into the foreground an attack on ethics, which knows no boundaries.[89] Grundmann's understanding of Jude's "faith" is therefore linked to life under the binding order of God where there is not just freedom from something, but also freedom to do something.[90] The issue at hand is behavior not doctrine.

In terms of the evaluative model therefore, Grundmann emphasizes Jude's perception of the situation that understands a significant threat to the community stemming from ungodly behavior, linked to a misunderstanding of Paul's gospel of freedom. While this behavior might be linked to a specific doctrine (perhaps coming out of Hellenistic-Jewish Wisdom traditions), the behavioral threat is so severe that the author limits the argument to simple ethical reproach. This makes Jude a situationist who offers a particular judgment without sound proofs.

While there is much that is attractive about Grundmann's approach, it would be stronger if more emphasis were given to Jude's ground of meaning beliefs. Grundmann allows his articulation of Jude's perception of the situation to guide his interpretation. His focus on Jude as a Jewish Christian arguing for the importance of ethics gives no attention to the important task of establishing the author's ground of meaning beliefs.

Other recent treatments of the Epistle of Jude continue to emphasize Jude's perception of the situation in their approach to the interpretation of the letter. Henning Paulsen, *Der Zweite Petrusbrief und der Judasbrief*, and Anton Vögtle, *Der Judasbrief, Der Zweite Petrusbrief*, demonstrate a continuing tendency to focus on a determination of Jude's perception of the situation.[91] Moreover, they represent a renewed commitment to maintaining an ecclesiastical or "early Catholic" characterization for the Epistle of Jude. While Ellis, Rowston, Grundmann and Bauckham forcefully argue for a characterization of Jude as a fairly early letter within a Jewish Christian milieu, Paulsen and Vögtle hold that Jude is a rather late letter that demonstrates the development of ecclesiastical or "early Catholic" elements.[92]

Vögtle is particularly concerned to counter the interpretations which emphasize Jude's concern for ethics as over against Jude's concern for orthodoxy.[93] At the heart of Vögtle's discussion lies his concern for an understanding of "faith" as doctrine. For Vögtle, the author of Jude perceives of a situation in which the "faith" is threatened by nonconformists who have an enthusiastic awareness of their possessing the Spirit, and feel a particular exemption from moral pressure.[94] Vögtle's emphasis is clearly on Jude as "...a distinct model of polemic against heresy in the early church."[95] This ecclesiastical or "early Catholic" characterization of the Epistle of Jude suggests that in addition to fitting the criteria of an interpretation which emphasizes Jude's perception of the situation, Vögtle might also be evaluated as an interpretation which is built around Jude's ecclesiastical or "early Catholic" ground of meaning beliefs.

Those interpretations which emphasize Jude's perception of the situation maintain the commitment to establishing a situation specific identification for the letter. This effort to establish the concrete historical situation behind the letter stems directly from the historical-critical treatments of the late nineteenth and early twentieth centuries. While many recent treatments establish a historical situation for the Epistle of Jude distinct from the ecclesiastical or "early Catholic" view of the letter taken in older treatments (e.g., Rowston's Palestinian Jewish-Christian Apocalyptic; Grundmann's emphasis on Jude as a Jewish-Christian letter primarily concerned with ethics), the interpretations of Paulsen and Vögtle demonstrate that this view is still prevalent within scholarship.

Jude and Loyalties, Interests, and Trusts

This group of critical variables provides the opportunity to evaluate interpretations of Jude's ethical admonition at three primary levels: (1) the loyalties, interests, and trusts of the scholar in question; (2) the faith dimension; and (3) group loyalties and ultimate values demonstrated in the text.

First, the discussion of the interpretations of Martin Luther and John Calvin reveals the need to recognize how a scholar's personal loyalties, interests, and trusts can influence the direction of interpretation. To be sure, all of the individuals examined could be critiqued at this level. Commitment to a specific methodology, or a particular philosophical framework often reveals more about the scholar in question than the interpretation yielded. Luther and Calvin allowed particular theological views to color their interpretation of the nature and purpose of Jude. Scholars in the late nineteenth and early twentieth centuries allowed particular philosophical frameworks (e.g., Hegelian dialectics), or critical presuppositions (e.g., the priority of 2 Peter) to determine their interpretation of the text. In recent years, commitment to a particular methodological approach (e.g., rhetorical or literary criticism) has often forced scholars to maintain a rigid consistency which does not allow for a more integrative approach to the question.

Second, the question of how a particular interpretation understands the nature of faith falls under the category of loyalties, interests, and trusts. Stassen argues that there is a need to distinguish "...between faith as personal trust and belief as doctrinal affirmation."[96] Is "faith" in the Epistle of Jude objective or subjective? How are faith-loyalties connected to ground of meaning beliefs? Are faith-loyalties consistent with or in conflict with ground of meaning beliefs? These are the questions which drive the faith dimension, and the faith dimension is of vital importance for a proper understanding of ethical admonition in the Epistle of Jude.

These questions, however, have not come to the fore in the preceding analysis of the interpretation of Jude's ethical admonition. The importance of a proper understanding of Jude's conception of faith is clear; however, when scholars do offer a judgment about the nature of "faith" in the Epistle of Jude, that judgment is usually presuppositional rather than conclusive. In other words, scholars make a judgment about what "faith" means for Jude, and then proceed with their interpretation based on that presupposition. For example, scholars who resonate with the "early Catholic" position define faith as doctrine and interpret Jude as a polemic against heresy. Faith-loyalties are discussed only as they relate to Jude's perception of the situation. The evaluative model suggests that faith-loyalties should stem from ground of meaning beliefs and influence how the situation is perceived.

Third, the loyalties, interests, and trusts quadrant deals with group loyalties and ultimate centers of value. Determining group loyalties and identifying centers of value is essentially a sociological task. Recently, Jerome Neyrey, *Jude, 2 Peter*, has provided significant insight into the sociological and anthropological criteria which are pertinent to the study of the Epistle of Jude.[97] In addition, Neyrey leans heavily on the tools of rhetorical analysis in his approach to both Jude and 2 Peter. Neyrey refers to his approach as "a new scholarly perspective" which includes the use of "...a number of social science models or perspectives to interpret Jude and 2 Peter."[98] Neyrey employs "five distinctive social science models" in his analysis of Jude and 2 Peter: (1) Honor and Shame as Pivotal Values; (2) Patron and Client Relationships; (3) Purity and Pollution: the Symbolic Universe of the Ancients; (4) the Physical Body; and (5) Group-oriented Person, not Modern Individualist.[99]

Neyrey applies these categories to the text of the Epistle of Jude and draws conclusions about the nature and purpose of the letter. Of utmost importance for Neyrey is the principle of Honor and Shame. Neyrey emphasizes those elements in the text which point to Jude's honor being challenged and defended. He argues that "the document may profitably be examined as the author's riposte to an honor challenge."[100] The writer of Jude establishes his authoritative status (v. 1), characterizes the ones making the honor challenge in terms of purity versus pollution (vv. 5–19), and maintains God as patron deserving of honor (vv. 24–25).

Neyrey clearly focuses on a determination of Jude's relative position and status within the group (group loyalties), and on Jude's ultimate center of value (a defence against an honor challenge). In this, Neyrey provides keen insight into the social forces that helped to drive the ethical argument in the Epistle of Jude. Of particular significance is Neyrey's identification of the social location of the author.[101] Here, Neyrey allows his conclusions about Jude's perception of the situation to flow from a determination of Jude's loyalties, interests, and trusts. In doing so, Neyrey follows the progression suggested by the evaluative model.

The perception of the situation is deeply influenced by individual loyalties, interests, and trusts. By establishing Jude's loyalties, interests and trusts through the sociological categories of honor/shame, patron/client, and purity/pollution, Neyrey grounds his conclusions about Jude's perception of the situation in the group loyalties and ultimate values which are identified in the text. Historical-critical approaches to the text endeavor to establish the perception of the situation first, and subsequently define group loyalties and ultimate values. Jude represents an "early Catholic" position, therefore, the author's ultimate value is "faith" as doctrine in need of defence. In contrast, Neyrey holds that honor, purity, and patronage are of ultimate value for the writer of Jude, and he argues that the writer of Jude perceives of a situation in which honor is challenged, purity is threatened, and patronage ignored. This is the clear strength of Neyrey's approach.

The weakness of Neyrey's approach is that it does not give enough attention to how Jude's ground of meaning beliefs help to shape and determine Jude's faith-loyalties. The gap between these two critical variables is admittedly quite narrow. Stassen acknowledges that some ethicists argue that faith-loyalties be subsumed to ground of meaning beliefs; however, faith-loyalties can either be consistent with ground of meaning beliefs or be in conflict with ground of meaning beliefs.[102] In either case, a determination of ground of meaning beliefs helps to inform the discussion of faith-loyalties.

In contrast, Neyrey allows various sociological categories to determine his identification of Jude's loyalties, interests, and trusts. Jude values honor because honor and shame has been identified as an important sociological category in the first century world.[103] While this is most certainly true, Jude's ground of meaning beliefs might point to another set of ultimate values and group loyalties.

Jude and the Ground of Meaning

While most recent studies of the Epistle of Jude emphasize a particular literary method, employ a sociological approach, or hold to a specific philosophical bias, a few scholars have sought to ground their interpretation of Jude's ethical admonition in the establishment of Jude's ground of meaning beliefs. In 1983, Richard Bauckham produced a ground breaking commentary on Jude and 2 Peter, and in recent years he has continued to illuminate the theological significance of the Epistle of Jude.[104] Bauckham's approach to the Epistle of Jude is significant because he successfully refutes the "early Catholic" characterization of the letter which dominates much of previous scholarship.[105] Moreover, Bauckham accomplishes this task by establishing

Jude's ground of meaning beliefs within an apocalyptic worldview.

Bauckham emphasizes Jude's strongly Jewish character and points to the elements in the letter which specifically reveal an apocalyptic Jewish-Christianity.[106] Bauckham resonates with Rowston's characterization of Jude's use of an apocalyptic worldview to bring about change within the community; however, Bauckham suggests that:

> Jude does not assert apocalyptic eschatology against denials of it. He takes
> it for granted and assumes his readers will. *It is the worldview within which*
> *he naturally thinks.*[107]

Jude's apocalyptic worldview—his apocalyptic ground of meaning— provides the foundation for Bauckham's interpretation of the letter.

Where other scholars hold Jude's description of God's judgment (vv. 5–19) to be the primary message of the letter, Bauckham understands the strong central section of the letter to provide "…essential background, but only background to the appeal" (vv. 3, 20–23).[108] The central section points to the certainty of God's judgment on ungodly individuals and "…is intended to persuade [Jude's] readers of the danger they face if they succumb to the libertine teaching and examples of the false teachers."[109] Bauckham establishes a ground of meaning for Jude in which the motivation to ethics stems from understanding God's judgments in history. The certainty of God's judgment prophesied by both Old Testament prophets, and apocalyptic writers provides Jude's motivation to ethics. Immoral, unethical behavior has always been punished. It will continue to be punished.

Out of this primary ground of meaning belief, Bauckham builds his full interpretation. Jude's loyalties, interests, and trusts, includes a view of faith as the content of the gospel which holds both the motivation and content of ethics: "…the message which demands faith."[110] God's action within history requires the human response of faith. Jude's group loyalties are to the community threatened by the false teachers. Ultimate value is placed on moral, or ethical behavior within that community.

Jude perceives of a situation in which that ultimate value is being threatened by false teachers who exhibit ethical libertinism. Bauckham dismisses attempts to make Jude's scathing attack on the behavior of these libertines a simple rhetorical argument. He states:

This attack on his opponents' morals is not a polemical device for slandering people with whom he disagreed on purely doctrinal grounds. On the contrary, it is precisely their ethical libertinism to which he objects.[111]

The nature of the perceived threat is behavioral and the degree of the threat is severe. Significantly, Bauckham does not link the threat to a specific heresy, or misunderstood Pauline theology. Rather, Bauckham argues that scholars far too often read Gnostic, or Pauline concepts into Jude, and therefore reach a false conclusion about Jude's perception of the situation. Bauckham suggests:

Once the attempt to read such clearly Gnostic ideas into Jude is given up, we are left with a picture of the opponents as charismatics who, on the basis of their understanding of grace, rejected all moral constraint and authority... At most the antinomianism of Jude's opponents was one of the streams which flowed into later Gnosticism.[112]

Bauckham's emphasis on Jude's concern for ethical, and moral relationships between members of the community allows for a perception of the situation which realizes "...the dispute between Jude and his opponents was not concerned with orthodoxy and heresy in belief, but with the relationship between the Gospel and moral obligation."[113]

Bauckham's description of Jude's mode of moral discourse stems from the articulation of Jude's apocalyptic worldview (Jude's ground of meaning beliefs). The polemical middle section of the letter (vv. 5–19) provides "exegetical background" to the main appeal set forth in verse 3 and continued in verses 20–23.[114] Bauckham essentially describes Jude as a principlist who applies principles to a situation which requires an ethical stance.

Bauckham's approach to the Epistle of Jude roughly corresponds to the processes which are outlined by the evaluative model. He establishes Jude's ground of meaning (e.g., an apocalyptic worldview), focuses on Jude's perception of the situation (a behavioral threat linked to the values which stem from the stated ground of meaning), and articulates Jude's mode of moral discourse (an exegetical application of principles to a new situation). Bauckham provides significant insight into Jude's ethical admonition; yet the well established scholarly characterization of Jude's negative thrust is only slightly diminished by Bauckham. Bauckham points to Jude's "…genuinely Christian pastoral concern for the reclamation of even the most obstinate."[115] The primary emphasis, however, continues to rest on God's condemnation of the opponents as motivation for the faithful to behave ethically.

One other aspect of Bauckham's approach to the Epistle of Jude requires brief attention. Bauckham maintains for Jude a significant place in the developing theology of the early Christian community.[116] Significantly, Bauckham distances Jude's theological reflection from Pauline theological reflection. Where Rowston, Vögtle, and a host of nineteenth and twentieth century scholars see strong links to Pauline language and concepts, Bauckham argues for a theological location contemporary with Paul in which both writers "…took over a great deal from the common tradition of primitive Christianity."[117]

Like Douglas Rowston, Roman Heiligenthal, *Zwischen Henoch und Paulus: Studien zum theologiegeschichtlichen Ort des Judasbriefes*, argues that the Epistle of Jude stands as a corrective to heretical doctrine stemming from a misunderstanding of Paul.[118] In contrast to Rowston, however, Heiligenthal allows his assessment of Jude's perception of the situation to flow from an attempt to establish Jude's ground of meaning beliefs.

Heiligenthal points to the strengthened interest in the Epistle of Jude, and calls for a changed view of the theological placement of the letter within the development of the early Christian community. In calling for a more serious examination of the theological significance of the letter, Heiligenthal hopes that Jude can move out of its "shadowy existence" and shed its "lump sum conviction" as mere polemic.[119]

To that end, Heiligenthal seeks to establish the theological location of the letter of Jude in relation to the theological development after Paul and in relation to several specific theological constructs. Heiligenthal suggests that Jude's use of Jewish apocalyptic literature, particularly *1 Enoch*, points to a specific theological background for the author of Jude. In addition, Heiligenthal argues that the author's reverence towards angels, and the christological and ecclesiological conceptions revealed in the letter can give important references to the place of the letter within the early Christian *Theologiegeschichte*.[120]

At the heart of Heiligenthal's assessment of the Epistle of Jude is his assertion that theological development after Paul can be subdivided into *assimilationsfreundliche* and *assimilationsfeindliche*.[121] Heiligenthal argues that friendly assimilation tendencies should be seen against a Hellenistic background, and that hostile assimilation tendencies should be seen against a Jewish-Christian background. With these broad categories in mind, Heiligenthal proceeds to identify the major theological positions expressed in the letter of Jude.

The letter speaks to a particular situation, from a particular point of view, with a particular set of theological or ground of meaning beliefs. Heiligengthal states that the Epistle of Jude:

> ...represents a Jewish-Christianity which sees in Jesus the coming Kyrios, who forms with his angels and the community a community of "saints," which should keep itself free from all impurity. Angel instructions and views of purity are expressions of a pharisaic piety.[122]

Heiligenthal focuses on Jude's use of 1 Enoch, the emphasis on angels, the importance of purity, the stress on teaching authority and apocalyptic eschatology. Out of these theological—ground of meaning—beliefs, Heiligenthal builds his interpretation of Jude's perception of the situation, mode of moral discourse, and loyalties, interests, and trusts.

Heiligenthal identifies the Epistle of Jude as a Jewish-Christian letter which demonstrates *assimilationsfeindliche* tendencies. More specifically, Heiligenthal argues that this anti-assimilation tendency is most clearly associated with Diaspora Christian Pharisees who examined *Enoch* for essential parts of their tradition. These Christian Pharisees understood themselves to be "familia dei," and they organized themselves into *Lehrhauses* in an effort to establish ways to defend against the assimilation tendencies of Hellenistic Christians.[123]

Heiligenthal suggests that certain elements of Jude's theology are clearly representative of Diaspora Pharisees (e.g., authoritative teaching, angel power, regard for categories of purity, and apocalyptic eschatology). The clearly Christian elements of Jude's theology (e.g., Christology) originate in the broader Christian *theologiegeschichtlich* which Heiligenthal identifies as *"antiochenischen Normaltheologie."*[124] These ground of meaning beliefs become the foundation upon which Heiligenthal builds the remainder of his interpretation.

Jude's loyalties, interests, and trusts stem from established ground of meaning beliefs. Group loyalty is to the "familia dei," that group of individuals set apart by their "faith."[125] Elsewhere, Heiligenthal argues that:

> "Faith" means to join with a brother in community. Revealing "faith" as the possible social identification, which outwardly is the central distinctive criterion makes possible the definition of the milieu. The wisdom writings also hold for "faith" this central function of membership, of an almost ecclesiastical character.[126]

For Heiligenthal, Jude understands "faith" to be the "criterion of membership" (*Maßstab der Zugehörigkeit*). In this conception, faith is neither a doctrine in need of a defence, nor the simple content of the gospel proclamation. Rather, it is the social distinction which sets apart the "faith bearer." When described in this manner, faith becomes a sociological category rather than a theological construct.[127] By emphasizing the social dimension of faith, Heiligenthal goes beyond the debate over faith as doctrine verses faith as belief. This community is made up of "faith bearers" who are interested in the Enochic tradition and value teaching authority, angel power, purity, and apocalyptic eschatology.

These loyalties, interests, and trusts allow Heiligenthal to extrapolate Jude's perception of the situation. Teaching authority is challenged, angel reverence is ridiculed, laws of purity are violated. Jude's concern for purity suggests to Heiligenthal that the nature of the threat is immoral behavior which stems from the excesses of extreme Paulinism.[128] The degree of threat is severe for it threatens the community of "faith bearers." The threat is clearly linked to a misunderstanding of Pauline teaching. Authority is located within the teaching tradition of the apostles, the Old Testament, and Jewish apocalyptic literature. In particular, *Enoch* holds a special place of authority within the teaching houses of this community. At the end of his extensive description, Heiligenthal suggests a specific situation. Jude writes against the extremes of Paulinism begun at Colossae.

Jude's mode of moral discourse in turn stems from the writer's ground of meaning beliefs, loyalties, interests, and trusts applied to the perception of the situation. Heiligenthal argues that the writer of Jude goes about the task of protecting the community from assimilating influences by applying basic beliefs about eschatology, angels, authoritative teaching, and purity to the situation perceived.[129] By definition, the writer is a principlist or contextualist who applies basic beliefs or principles to the situation at hand.

Heiligenthal's interpretation demonstrates a remarkable adherence to the analytical processes which are described by the evaluative model. Heiligenthal establishes the writer's theological or ground of meaning beliefs, and then argues for particular loyalties, interests, and trusts, a specific perception of the situation, and a mode of moral discourse which is consistent with basic beliefs. While the content of Heiligenthal's conclusions may be criticized, the progression of his analysis conforms to the processes outlined by the evaluative model.[130]

Conclusion

The goal of this chapter was to provide a limited *Forschungsgeschichte* focused on the interpretation of Jude's ethical admonition. Adapting the critical variables articulated by Glen Stassen for the analysis of ethical decision making, chapter two established a model for the evaluation of how Jude's ethical admonitions have been interpreted. This chapter used the model to examine various interpretations of Jude throughout history.

It should be noted that the four quadrants of the evaluative model correspond roughly to the methodological approaches which have dominated the study of the New Testament over the last century. Scholars who focus on historical-critical studies are essentially concerned with establishing the perception of the situation demonstrated in the text. Sociological or anthropological methodologies deal primarily with establishing the loyalties, interests, and trusts which influence the interpretation of a particular text. Literary studies have emphasized the mode of moral discourse. The ground of meaning quadrant concerns itself with establishing the theological content of a particular text.

Each of these approaches provides insight into the purpose and message of the Epistle of Jude. They are, however, by their very nature, limited to examining *individual* variables that make up ethical argument and ethical admonition. A more fruitful approach to the interpretation of the ethical admonition in the Epistle of Jude would follow the integrative pattern established by the evaluative model by which the identification of Jude's perception of the situation, mode of moral discourse, and loyalties, interests, and trusts stems from an articulation of Jude's ground of meaning beliefs. Using the same organizational pattern articulated by Stassen it is possible to graphically demonstrate how previously divergent methodological approaches to the Epistle of Jude might relate to each other:

The Interpretation of Jude's Ethical Admonition

Perception of the Situation	Mode of Moral Discourse
Historical-Critical Approaches: Nineteenth and Twentieth Century Treatments Douglas Rowston Walter Grundmann Henning Paulsen (Anton Vögtle)	Literary-Critical Approaches: E. Earle Ellis Duane F. Watson J. Daryl Charles
Loyalties, Interests, and Trusts	**Ground of Meaning**
Sociological Approaches: Jerome Neyrey (Martin Luther)[131] (John Calvin)	Theological Approaches: Roman Heiligenthal Richard Bauckham (Anton Vögtle)

Fig. 11

Chapter four seeks to establish Jude's ground of meaning beliefs by examining the critical variables which form the content of the ground of meaning quadrant. Jude's motivation to ethics, the content of ethical obligation, the power to do ethics, and the agent or channel of ethics is related to Jude's understanding of God's action in history and the human response to God's action. This understanding of God's action and the human response to God's action is described in terms of Jude's apocalyptic worldview. More specifically, Jude's dynamic outlook can be discussed in terms of the tension between eschatology—God's action in history—and ecclesiology—the human response to God's action.

Chapter Four

Jude's Ground of Meaning

A proper understanding of the ethical admonition contained in the Epistle of Jude can only be achieved if there is an examination of the driving force behind the argument. Chapter three demonstrates the danger of placing too much emphasis on those critical variables which do not stand at the heart of the argument, but rather point to the mode of moral discourse, the perception of the situation, or the loyalties, interests, and trusts which affect the argument. What is absolutely vital in understanding the heart of ethical admonition is a proper understanding of what Stassen calls "the ground of meaning."

Stassen argues that the ground of meaning variable has to do fundamentally with the motivation to ethics, the content of ethical obligation, the source of power to do ethics, and the agent or channel of ethics.[1] An examination of how these variables relate to the Epistle of Jude will help to establish Jude's ground of meaning beliefs. To anticipate the argument, Jude's ground of meaning is best understood in terms of Jude's apocalyptic worldview. This is true because his apocalyptic worldview is linked to Jude's perception of God's action in history (the motivation to ethics) and Jude's perception of the human response to God's action in history (the content, power, and channel of ethics). An understanding of Jude's ground of meaning beliefs provides the foundation for an analysis of Jude's perception of the situation, mode of moral discourse, and loyalties, interests, and trusts.

Of paramount importance for establishing Jude's ground of meaning beliefs is an acceptance of the tension between eschatology—God's action in history—and ecclesiology—everyday living within the community.[2] This tension can be addressed by examining the content of Jude's ethical obligation, the power to do Jude's ethics, and the agent or channel of Jude's ethics in relation to Jude's motivation to ethics. At this point, the significant contribution of Christopher Rowland provides a very helpful starting point for understanding how apocalyptic functions both to shed light on the future and to demonstrate how individuals and groups with an apocalyptic worldview ought to behave in the here and now.[3]

By acknowledging the tension found in apocalyptic between eschatology and ecclesiology, it is possible to establish a model for interpreting Jude's ethical admonitions. The model takes as its foundation a ground of meaning set squarely within an apocalyptic worldview. In addition, it takes seriously the other critical variables which determine ethical argument and admonition. It holds together and illuminates the tension between eschatology and ecclesiology and demonstrates how the perception of the situation, loyalties and trusts, mode of moral discourse determine ethical admonition in the Epistle of Jude.

Apocalyptic as the Perception of God's Action in and Through History

At its core, apocalyptic speaks to how humanity perceives God's action in history, both in the past and in the future. This is the essential question for determining the motivation to ethics. In the face of what has been argued about how ethical admonition can and should be interpreted, the search for Jude's "ground of meaning" begins with an attempt to understand how apocalyptic and an apocalyptic worldview influence Jude's motivation to ethics.

The search for Jude's motivation to ethics in the milieu of apocalyptic and an apocalyptic worldview requires a brief discussion of the distinction between the genre apocalypse and apocalyptic worldview. While the Epistle of Jude in no way conforms to the genre of an apocalypse, many elements of the genre's definition are relevant for our understanding of Jude's ground of meaning. The distinction, however, between apocalypse as a unique genre and apocalyptic, or apocalypticism as a distinct worldview demonstrates the need to examine Jude's unique position as a "consumer" of apocalyptic ideas, concepts, and literature.

Jude's Motivation to Ethics

In his essay, "Apokalyptik und Ethik: Die Kategorie der Zukunft als Anweisung für sittliches Handeln," Joachim Gnilka articulates the significance of the relationship between ethical behavior and the Christian perception of God's action in history. Gnilka relates ethics both to the perception of God's action in the future and to the effects of God's action in the present. Gnilka writes:

The rule of God is not merely future eschatological hereafter (although it is primarily), on the contrary, it becomes effective even in this world by its healing and delivering power... So the impetus for ethical behavior remains upon the hopeful orientation of Christian existence toward this absolute future.[4]

Gnilka's observations point to the intimate connection between an apocalyptic worldview and ethics, where ethical behavior flows directly from an understanding of God's action in and through history.

The evaluative model confirms that the motivation to ethics arises primarily from the perception of God's action in human history. Jude's setting within the milieu of Palestinian Jewish Christianity strengthens the scholarly argument that Jude works within the rubric of apocalyptic to reach his didactic goals.[5] Jude's apocalyptic worldview informs our understanding of Jude's motivation to ethics within the broader perspective of Jude's ground of meaning beliefs.

In the New Testament Jude stands in the unique position of being a "consumer" of apocalyptic literature. The letter does not conform to the characteristics of the genre; however, it betrays distinct perspectives that are generally associated with apocalypses. In addition, Jude's use of particular Old Testament types (the Wilderness Generation, the Watchers, Sodom and Gomorrah, Cain, Balaam, Korah), and his citation or allusion to specific apocalyptic literature (The *Assumption of Moses, 1 Enoch*) reveals an intimate connection with an apocalyptic worldview. Jude's apocalyptic worldview, as demonstrated by his use of apocalyptic ideas, concepts and literature, provides a framework for establishing Jude's motivation to ethics within the broader concern of Jude's ground of meaning beliefs.

W. S. Vorster states that "...much of what we find in the New Testament is written from an apocalyptic eschatological perspective."[6] Vorster emphasizes the "eschatological" elements which most scholars recognize in apocalyptic writings. Efforts to redefine and reevaluate our understanding of the meaning of apocalyptic have led many scholars to draw fine distinctions between apocalypse as a genre, apocalyptic as a particular eschatological religious perspective, and apocalypticism as a sociological ideology.[7] Attempts to examine the genre and establish a definition have yielded significant results.[8]

Not every text which demonstrates "apocalyptic eschatology" can be seen as an apocalypse; however, the "…label 'apocalyptic eschatology' should be reserved for the eschatology found in apocalypses or *recognized by analogy with them*."[9] The eschatological perspective revealed in apocalypses shares two distinct characteristics with Jude's apocalyptic worldview: (1) the hope of eschatological judgment/destruction, and (2) the hope of eschatological salvation.[10]

Definitions of the genre allow for the identification and classification of texts as apocalypses; yet, offer not enough to help us understand the apocalyptic worldview which tends to produce such texts. Moreover, they do very little to increase our understanding about the consumers of such texts—a major consideration in the examination of the Epistle of Jude. In his assessment of the significance of apocalyptic for the Qumran community, William Beardslee points to the need to go beyond those texts which conform to the literary criteria of an apocalypse in the examination of what constitutes apocalyptic.[11] Texts that resonate with the themes established in apocalyptic literature, or which employ apocalyptic forms, motifs, or actual citations provide insight into the apocalyptic worldview that produces such texts.

An Apocalyptic Worldview. Mitchell Reddish suggests that "apocalyptic eschatology refers to a particular view of God's activity in the future."[12] Reddish distinguishes apocalyptic eschatology and apocalypse from the broader sociological perspective of apocalypticism:

> Apocalypticism is a pattern of thought or a worldview dominated by the kinds of ideas and motifs found in apocalypses—emphasis on other worlds (heaven, hell, the abode of the dead) and otherworldly beings (God, Satan, angels, demons), supernatural intervention in world events, apocalyptic eschatology, and divine retribution beyond death.[13]

An apocalyptic worldview is the way in which certain individuals and groups perceive of reality.[14] An apocalypse is the literary expression of that particular worldview.

Perhaps more helpful for the task of identifying Jude's ground of meaning beliefs is Vorster's argument against the notion of an apocalyptic genre in favor of an apocalyptic worldview.[15] Vorster argues from the idea of "text types" that there is in fact no distinct genre "apocalypse," but rather narrative texts and argumentative texts which express a particular worldview—namely, an apocalyptic-eschatological perspective. Jude is not an apocalypse, but the letter might helpfully be classified as an argumentative text which expresses an apocalyptic-eschatological perspective. While the Epistle of Jude does not fulfill the requirements of the genre apocalypse, the letter betrays an eschatological perspective which can be recognized by analogy with the eschatological perspective of much apocalyptic literature.

Jude as a "Consumer" of Apocalyptic. The clearest evidence of Jude's close relationship to the apocalyptic worldview expressed in apocalyptic literature is Jude's unique position as a consumer of apocalyptic. Jude's reference to *The Assumption of Moses*, his direct citation of *1 Enoch* 1:9, and the combination of Old Testament types referred to in the central section of the letter reveals Jude's unique perception of God's action in and through history.

The *Assumption of Moses*. The difficulty presented by any attempt to deal with the so-called *Assumption of Moses* is that it is not extant.[16] The portion in question—Jude's reference in verse nine—comes from the presumed lost ending of the *Assumption* which is sometimes called *The Testament of Moses*.[17] Johannes Tromp provides an excellent and detailed treatment of the critical issues surrounding the *Assumption of Moses*.[18] After examining recent treatments of the critical issues, Tromp offers his own conclusions about the title, date, origin and language, milieu, genre, literary integrity, and purpose of the *Assumption of Moses*. Tromp suggests that the *Assumption of Moses* should not be equated with the *Testament of Moses*, but rather it should be understood as a separate work.[19]

Tromp dates the writing in the early first century A.D., not long after the death of Herod the Great. Citing the work of D. M. Rhodes, Tromp argues that "the *Assumption* may bear witness to a spirit and a milieu which pervaded the Jewish nation from 4 B.C. to A.D. 48."[20] With regard to the origin and language of the *Assumption of Moses*, Tromp points to the emphasis on Jerusalem and the Temple cult revealed in the book; and, in addition, cites *Assumption* 1:4 where Aram is *trans Jordanean*, thus suggesting a Palestinian perspective.[21] While the only extant text is in Latin, Tromp argues that it is a translation from the Greek. Tromp does not rule out the possibility that the presumed Greek text was itself a translation from an original Hebrew text.[22]

In terms of genre, Tromp convincingly argues that the *Assumption of Moses* is in the form of a "farewell discourse."[23] This assessment of the literary form of the *Assumption of Moses* affects the interpretation of the "lost" ending of the *Assumption* cited in Jude 9. Bauckham attempts an extensive reconstruction of the story Jude cites in verse nine.[24] Tromp discounts Bauckham's detailed treatment of the sources which provides not one, but two possible "lost" endings. Tromp applies appropriate restraint in his treatment of the sources, and concludes that "…the reliable traces of *As. Mos.* in ecclesiastical literature are few, and…they allow only very modest conclusions with regard to the ending of this work.[25] The extant text is in the form of a Testament so some accounting of the end of Moses life could be expected. In addition, in 1:15 ("Therefore, I shall speak plainly to you. The years of my life have come to an end…") and 10:14 ("However, I shall sleep with my fathers") Moses expects death. Finally, in 11:7 (Or who as a man will dare to move your body from place to place?), Joshua alludes to angelic beings.[26] These factors suggest that the lost ending probably existed and contained an account of the argument of Michael the archangel with the Devil over the body of Moses.[27]

While Tromp's analysis of the critical issues surrounding the *Assumption of Moses* is excellent, it is his conclusion about the religious and cultural milieu which helped to produce the *Assumption* which is more pertinent in a search for Jude's ground of meaning. Tromp concludes that "…the author of *As. Mos.* belonged to a group in society with limited actual power."[28] Tromp does not place the burden of a specific political situation as the occasion for the production of the *Assumption of Moses*, but rather maintains the relative position of the author as one of powerlessness against any authority. This position of relative powerlessness demonstrates the necessity of the apocalyptic perception of God's action in history to judge the wicked and save the righteous. Because of the powerlessness of the individual or group, emphasis is placed on God's role as judge.

Jude's reference to the story of the debate between Michael and the Devil resonates with this emphasis on judgment belonging to God and God alone. Jude's recollection of the story emphasizes the archangel Michael's deference in acknowledging that judgment or rebuke belongs to God alone: He did not dare to pronounce a blaspheming judgment, but he said, "The Lord rebuke you!" (οὐκ ἐτόλμησεν κρίσεν ἐπενεγκεῖν βλασφημίας ἀλλὰ εἶπεν,

Ἐπιτιμήσαι σοι κύριος).[29] Disputes over the translation of κρίσεν...βλασφημίας aside, the recollection of the story provides stark evidence that the role of judge belongs solely to God. With this reminder, Jude begins to reveal a key component in his perception of God's action in history. Even the angels cannot act alone to judge. Judgment belongs to God alone.

1 Enoch **1:9.** The citation of *1 Enoch* 1:9 provides Jude's clearest connection to apocalyptic literature and an apocalyptic worldview. While the entire letter is replete with allusions and references to both the Old Testament and other non-canonical writings, the reference to Enoch's prophecy (vv. 14–15) is Jude's only explicit citation. Like Jude's recollection of the story from the *Assumption of Moses*, the citation of *1 Enoch* 1:9 functions to punctuate the idea that judgment belongs to God alone.

The use and preservation of *1 Enoch* by the early Christian community is well documented, and clearly the book played an important role in the theological reflection of the early church.[30] Origen refers to "Enoch's book" (*De Princ.* 4:1:35; *C. Cels.* 5:54). Tertullian argues for the genuineness of Enoch's prophecy by pointing to the citation in Jude 14–15 (*Ap. of Women* 1:3). Anatolius of Alexandra uses "the book of Enoch" to prove an argument about the dating of the first month among the Hebrews (*Paschal Canon*, 5).[31]

Beyond the references to Enoch's writing, the figure of Enoch held some significance for the early Christian community (1 Clement 10; Irenaeus, *Against Heresies* 4:16:2, 5:5:1; Tertullian, *On the Resurrection of Flesh*, 58). Enoch and Enoch's book also figure prominently in the *Testaments of the Twelve Patriarchs* (*T. Simeon* 5; *T. Levi* 5, 10, 16; *T. Judah* 38; *T. Zeb.* 3; *T. Napt.* 4; *T. Benj.* 9–10; *T. Abraham* B, 11). At least initially, the early Christian community held few reservations about the use of the figure Enoch and the writings produced in his name.[32]

Since the discovery of fragments from *1 Enoch* at Qumran, the scholarly world has had to reassess the significance of *1 Enoch* and the worldview it represents. All of the sections of the Ethiopic text are represented in the Aramaic fragments except chapters 37–71, the *Similitudes*.[33] While significant debate about the date and provenance of the *Similitudes* continues, conclusions about the origin of Jude's citation in verses 14–15 are more certain.[34]

Jude's citation comes from *1 Enoch* 1:1–9, from the section of *1 Enoch* called *The Book of the Watchers* (chapters 1–36). These chapters are reasonably dated to the second or third century B.C.[35]   In addition, early themes, thought patterns, and modes of expression may have been set before the completion of the final form of the book.[36]   *The Book of the Watchers* can be divided into three subsections: (1) chapters 1–5, introduction; (2) chapters 6–16, an elaboration of Genesis 6:1–4; and (3) Enoch's cosmic journey to the far ends of the earth.[37]   Jude certainly demonstrates familiarity with the introductory chapters (Jude 14–15), and his knowledge of the Watcher story betrays indebtedness to the Enochic elaboration.[38]

Apart from arguments about the date and provenance of the extant text, "…the real importance of Enoch does not lie in the fact that it is a 'lost' Jewish text preserved only by Christian hands…, [but] it lies in the questions raised by the book and the worldview it presents."[39]   The emphasis in *1 Enoch* rests on the realization of God's righteous judgment. The figure Enoch relates "a holy vision from the heavens" in which "the God of the universe, the Holy Great One, will come forth from his dwelling….and there shall be judgment upon all, (including) the righteous" (1:2–7).   *1 Enoch* 1:9 follows the assurances given to the righteous:

> And to all the righteous he will grant peace. He will preserve the elect, and kindness shall be upon them. They shall all belong to God and they shall prosper and be blessed; and the light of God shall shine unto them (1:8).

In contrast to the assurances made to the righteous concerning their state of preservation, 1:9 offers equal assurance to the wicked concerning their state of judgment:

> Behold, he will arrive with ten million of the holy ones in order to execute judgment upon all. He will destroy the wicked ones and censure all flesh on account of everything that they have done, that which the sinners and the wicked ones committed against him (1:9).

The Watcher angels are portrayed as the ultimate type of rebellious sinner, and chapters 6–12 relate their disobedience and God's action to pronounce judgment upon them. Significantly, chapters 12–16 relate how "…the evil Watchers ask Enoch to intercede for them with God."[40] Subsequently, Enoch receives instructions from God to pronounce judgment on the Watchers; yet, he continues in his capacity as intercessor, leaving the judgment of sinners to God. Enoch's intercession includes production of a record of sinful behavior in a petition, and delivery of said petition to the Lord (13:4–7). The Watchers story betrays a worldview which understands God—and God alone—acting to judge the sin of the unrighteous. Moreover, it presents a righteous one (Enoch) acting in the role of intercessor for the unrighteous.

As with the recollection of the story from the *Assumption of Moses*, Jude's citation of *1 Enoch* 1:9 functions to articulate Jude's perception of God's action in and through history. God alone has authority to judge the wicked. Judgment may be announced by heralds (Michael, Enoch), or enjoined by "myriads of holy ones," but the act of judging belongs to God alone. Jude's use of apocalyptic traditions provides striking punctuation to the exegetical exposition of Jude's perception of God's action in and through history as portrayed in several Old Testament types.

The Old Testament Types. Jude's use of the Old Testament is limited to allusions, reminiscences, and catchwords.[41] J. Daryl Charles asserts that "while not a single explicit citation from the OT is found in Jude, the brief epistle nonetheless is replete with examples of prophetic typology."[42] The letter demonstrates "astounding verbal brevity" and "a comprehensive knowledge and calculated use of the OT."[43] Bauckham argues that in spite of Jude's good grasp of the Greek language "at no point where he alludes to specific verses of the OT does he echo the language of the LXX."[44] Rowston suggests Jude's "dependence upon the Old Testament could be of a direct or indirect nature," and he holds open the position that Jude could be citing the OT directly, or calling upon Jewish interpretation of scripture.[45]

Jude's use of OT types emphasizes his perception of God's action in and through history, which in turn provides the foundation for Jude's motivation to ethics. Ellis emphasizes Jude's commentary pattern and points to Jude's alternation of Old Testament passages with commentary on the present situation.[46] Since Ellis' essay, commentators have emphasized Jude's careful exegesis of the Old Testament and Jewish apocalyptic literature to make a clear-cut case against the false teachers in the community. While essentially correct, the interpretive emphasis should be shifted from judgment of the false teachers to Jude's articulation of God—and God alone—acting to judge.

Jude begins his argument with a trio of images which stress the culpability of rebellious groups (vv. 5–7). Moreover, Jude draws "…on a traditional schema in which such examples were listed."[47]   Bauckham states that "the main context of the traditional schema was Jewish paraenesis in which the hearers were warned not to follow these examples."[48]   Here, Jude "...*interprets* the tradition as typological prophecy of the false teachers and their coming judgment."[49]

Verse 5 introduces the image of the children of Israel who were delivered out of Egypt only to be destroyed because of their unbelief.   Other New Testament books pick up this warning image (1 Cor 10:5, Heb 4:7ff).[50] Despite textual difficulties, Jude emphasizes God's action in history to judge rebellious sinners.[51] Interestingly, the Lord both saves ([ὁ]κύριος ἅπαξ λαὸν ἐκ γῆς Αἰγύπτου σώσας) and judges (τὸ δεύτερον τοὺς μὴ πιστεύσαντας ἀπώλεσεν).   The presentation of Jude's perception of God's action in and through history begins with a remembrance of God's acting both to save and to judge.

Verse 6 introduces the tradition found in Gen 6:1–4 which speaks of the "sons of God" taking "daughters of men."   Tord Fornburg holds that "some details in Jude v. 6 are missing there [Gen 6:1–4], but are to be found in, e.g., *1 Enoch*."[52] Jude expands the allusion to the OT tradition by using additional material from *1 Enoch*.[53]   The identity of the sinners changes from "sons of God" to "angels."   Jude articulates the nature of their "sin" and defines it as "abandonment of their appointed place."   Finally, Jude describes their punishment (εἰς κρίσιν μεγάλης ἡμέρας δεσμοῖς ἀϊδίοις ὑπὸ ζόφον τετήρηκεν).[54]   Jude's description of their punishment as "have been kept" draws a comparison to the status of the community addressed in verse 1 (τοῖς ἐν θεῷ πατρὶ ἠγαπημένοις καὶ Ἰησοῦ Χριστῷ τετηρημένοις κλητοῖς), and it reveals an important aspect of Jude's perception of God's action in history. All individuals—both righteous and unrighteous—are kept until the "great day of judgment."

Verse 7 completes the trilogy of examples by citing Sodom and Gomorrah (Gen 19), "...the classic Jewish example of immorality."[55]   While some commentators argue that the emphasis here is clearly on sexual sin as distinct from the usurping of authority which is implicit in verse 6, Bauckham points out that "in Jewish tradition the sin of Sodom was rarely specified as homosexual practice....the incident with the angels is usually treated as a violation of hospitality."[56] No matter the nature of the sin characterized by Sodom and Gomorrah, Jude's emphasis is on God's unique role as judge.   As in the two previous examples, Jude stresses the judgment of God, and God alone.

In verse 8 Jude argues that like the groups of old, the troublemakers in the community "pollute their own bodies, reject authority, and slander celestial beings" (NIV). In like manner, these dissidents are worthy of the same righteous judgment that God brought to the wilderness generation, the Watchers, and the cities of Sodom and Gomorrah. Yet, Jude himself does not offer words of condemnation. Rather, verse 9 provides a powerful punctuation to the three OT examples. While these sinners are worthy of judgment, it is God—and God alone—who will act to judge them.

In verse 11 "Cain, Balaam, and Korah are united by means of a woe-oracle."[57] Cain is mentioned first, and the obvious reference is to Gen 4:3–8, but "…dependence is from Jude to the Old Testament through first century Judaism."[58] Sidebottom points out that "Cain appears as the murderer (and so the man of unrighteousness) *par excellence*," in Jewish writing (Wis 10:3; *1 Enoch, T. Abraham*; 1 John 3:12).[59] Kelly cites Philo's characterization of Cain as "…a great lover of self, the rebel against God who relies on his own resources."[60] Josephus (*Ant.* 1.52–66) similarly "…treats [Cain] as the embodiment of violence and lust, greed and blasphemy in general."[61] It seems clear that "to the Jewish mind, Cain represents the epitome of wickedness…the 'type' and 'teacher' of ungodliness."[62]

The prophet Balaam is mentioned second in verse 11. Rowston states that "there seems to have been two different traditions about Balaam….the favorable one of Numbers 22–24…[and] the unfavorable tradition of Numbers 31:16."[63] In the later tradition, which is picked up by Jude, "Balaam was represented…as a false teacher leading the Israelites into licentiousness for gain."[64] In Jude's exegesis Balaam is "…the prototype of unprincipled people who will not shrink from any enormity for monetary gain and who, like him are doomed to hell."[65]

The third figure in verse 11 is the Israelite Korah. Korah's OT story is found in Numbers 16 and 26:10. Korah and his rebellious followers are "…counted as flagrant examples of blasphemous insubordination and or the swift penalty awaiting it."[66] Bauckham states that Korah "…became the classic example of the antinomian heretic."[67] Bauckham outlines the development of this tradition by citing the extrabiblical evidence which links Korah's rebellion with specific complaints and offence against Moses and the

Torah.[68]

While this second group of OT examples provides Jude's more specific charges against the opponents, it is also concerned to place God and God alone in the role of judge. Bauckham argues that the most likely sense of ὅτι τῇ ὁδῷ τοῦ Κάϊν ἐπορεύθησαν is that Jude's opponents "…have followed in Cain's footsteps by imitating his sin."[69] Jude certainly wishes to point out the sin of his opponents; however, the judgment which God brought to Cain cannot have been completely removed from the mind of Jude's recipients. In the same way, τῇ πλάνῃ τοῦ Βαλαὰμ μισθοῦ ἐξεχύθησαν sharpens and defines the nature of the troublemakers sin, but it also recalls the judgment which Balaam received from God. Finally, with τῇ ἀντιλογίᾳ τοῦ Κόρε ἀπώλοντο Jude provides explicit reference to God's judgment.[70]

Jude's use of OT types, particularly when seen in conjunction with the punctuating stories from *As. Mos.* and *1 Enoch*, reveals how Jude perceives of God's action in and through history: God—and God alone—acts to judge the sinful acts of groups and individuals. God judged the Wilderness generation. God judged the Watchers. God judged Sodom and Gomorrah. Yet, even the archangel Michael did not dare to judge the devil. Judgment belongs to God alone. Cain, Balaam, and Korah provide more substance to Jude's charges, but their judgment also belongs to God. Jude's motivation to ethics, therefore, is directly linked to the understanding of God consistently acting to judge sinful behavior.

Jude's emphasis on God's judgment reveals one half of his perception of God's action in history and is readily apparent in the text. While Jude's treatment of God's saving action in history is less prominent, it is certainly no less foundational to his ground of meaning beliefs. Jude may have wished to write a more substantial treatment of God's saving activity, but the problems which faced his community demanded a more focused approach (v. 3). Yet, underlying the whole of Jude's argument is the understanding that God in Jesus Christ has acted to save. In verse one, Jude writes τοῖς ἐν θεῷ πατρὶ ἠγαπημένοις καὶ Ἰησοῦ Χριστῷ τετηρημένοις κλητοῖς. An understanding of God's saving action in Jesus Christ is presumed among the recipients of the letter. Verse 3 speaks of τῆς κοινῆς ἡμῶν σωτηρίας as the basis for fellowship, and stands as Jude's primary concern. Verse 21 urges the members of the community to προσδεχόμενοι τὸ ἔλεος τοῦ κυρίου ἡμῶν

'Ιησοῦ Χριστοῦ, and verses 24–25 remind the reader that glory, majesty, power and authority belong μόνῳ θεῷ σωτῆρι ἡμῶν διὰ Ἰησοῦ Χριστοῦ τοῦ κυρίου ἡμῶν.

Jude's motivation to ethics relates directly to his perception of God's action in and through history both to judge and to save. The human response to God's action in history makes up the content of ethics. The power to do ethics and the channel of ethics also stem from the human perception of how God acts in and through history. Jude's apocalyptic worldview points to his perception of God's action in history, but it also provides insight into how apocalyptic functions as a principle for organizing community life. Jude's ground of meaning holds together the tension between God's action in history to judge and to save, and the need to live together in community.

Apocalyptic as a Principle for Organizing Community Life

Wayne Meeks points to several characteristics which would be readily apparent in "...any literature we would call 'apocalyptic.'"[71] Chief among these characteristics for Meeks is the division of the world into cosmic, temporal, and social dualities. Meeks is primarily concerned with demonstrating the social function of apocalyptic language in the writings of Paul.[72] This effort to understand the social function of apocalyptic in the New Testament is often subsumed to the study of the cosmic, or temporal dualities within apocalyptic.[73] To his credit, Meeks emphasizes the importance of the present social situation for apocalyptic interpretation of scripture:

> For the apocalyptic interpreter, the present moment and his own sect are the focus of all revelation. All that is past is prologue to what is about to happen; all that has been written and spoken in the sacred tradition was pointing to this group and this time.[74]

In spite of Meeks' emphasis, "...concentration on the future orientation of the apocalypses has at times given a rather distorted view of the essence of apocalyptic."[75]

Christopher Rowland offers a helpful corrective to this misplaced emphasis by suggesting that scholarship approach apocalyptic without emphasizing the eschatological elements. For Rowland, "apocalyptic is a much involved in the attempt to understand things as they are now as to predict future events."[76] This is significant for our understanding of Jude's ground of meaning beliefs because Jude is particularly concerned with "understanding things as they are now." Rowland contends:

> the key to the whole movement [apocalyptic] is that God reveals his mysteries directly to man and thereby gives them knowledge of the true nature of reality so that they may *organize their lives accordingly.*[77]

Rowland's contention allows Jude, as a consumer of apocalyptic ideas, concepts, and literature, to demonstrate an apocalyptic worldview which is not primarily concerned with eschatological events. On the contrary, Jude's ethical admonitions are grounded in his perception of God's revealed action in history.

Certainly Jude displays a keen interest in the Parousia, but there is also a concern for the organization of life based on the divinely revealed nature of reality. When eschatology is not the distinguishing feature of apocalyptic, we see that Jude is more concerned with demonstrating the certainty of God's action in history both to judge and to save. In addition, Jude admonishes the faithful to organize their lives in accordance with this divine reality and instructs the community in how to complete this task. Jude's concern with God's action in and through history—eschatology— informs our understanding of Jude's motivation to ethics. Jude's concern with organizing community life—ecclesiology—informs our understanding of the content of Jude's ethic, the power to do Jude's ethic, and the channel of Jude's ethic.

The Content of Jude's Ethic

The content of ethical admonition is centered in the human response to the perception of God's action in and through history. The human response to God's action in history has created a situation where individuals are "kept" and "called" into community with God and each other by the saving work of God in Jesus Christ (Jude 1, 24–25). Interestingly for Jude, the state of "being kept" is one that applies to both the faithful and the unfaithful. Commentators point to the "catchword" connections, and the word play on τηρεῖν in verses 1, 6, 13, 21; however, for Jude the human state of "being kept" is less an argumentative device than a statement of his perception of reality.[78]

Jude writes to a community "kept in Jesus Christ" (v. 1), and he urges them to "keep yourselves in the love of God" (v. 21). In contrast, the Watchers are "kept until the great day of Judgment" (v. 6), and comparatively, the troublemakers are "kept in the gloom of darkness forever" (v. 13). The positive, or faithful response to God's saving action in and through history allows an individual to be kept by God "in the mercy of our Lord Jesus Christ" (v. 21) in anticipation of the moment when he or she can stand blameless before his glory (vv. 24–25). The negative, or rebellious response to God's saving action in history leads to the state of being kept in judgment.

In the juxtaposition of these two extremes, the content of Jude's ethic becomes evident. All humanity is kept either in mercy or in judgment. From the divine perspective, these judgments have been prescribed from long ago (v. 4, οἱ πάλαι προγεγραμμένοι εἰς τοῦτο τὸ κρίμα). Jude, however, understands that judgment belongs to God, and God alone. Human participation in the action of God in and through history is limited to demonstrations of mercy (vv. 22–23; Cf. 2 Pet 1:4). The content of Jude's ethic—the human response to God's action in history—is twofold. Moral behavior is expected, but when individuals and groups within the community are found wanting in this area, their judgment should be left to God. The community should strive to demonstrate mercy even as mercy has been demonstrated to them. This mandate to demonstrate mercy holds together the channel of Jude's ethic and the power to do Jude's ethic.

The Channel of Jude's Ethic

The agent or channel of Jude's ethic is twofold. As has been demonstrated, Jude's motivation to ethics understands God and God alone to be the agent or channel of judgment. The community of believers, however, becomes the agent or channel of God's mercy. Verses 22–23 outline Jude's admonition to the community to be agents of God's mercy.[79] Jude admonishes the faithful to "be merciful to the ones who dispute; save some, snatching them out of the fire; to others be merciful in fear, hating even the garment stained by the flesh." At no point does Jude admonish the community to judge the sinners in their midst, but rather, he warns of the danger attached to such behavior and admonishes the faithful to demonstrate mercy in spite of the danger.

These verses resonate with Jude's address, and wish for the community he addresses: "May mercy, peace, and love be given you in abundance" (v. 2). Bauckham comments that "the salutation (v. 2) is somewhat closer than many other early Christian examples to Jewish forms....[and] originates from blessing formulae."[80] The greeting "peace" is typically Jewish, but Jude's incorporation of ἔλεος and particularly ἀγάπη is specifically Christian. While there are non-epistolary examples of the incorporation of mercy into a blessing, Jude's use of ἔλεος with the optative πλαθυνθείη in the salutation is unique in the NT.[81] Mercy stands second in the salutation triads of 1 Tim 1:2; 2 Tim 1:2; and 2 John 3. Moreover, Jude *wishes* that "mercy, peace, and love may increase."[82] Jude's use of the optative πληθυνθείη conforms to its use in other Jewish-Christian salutations which use it "...as a 'divine passive' to wish that God may give blessings abundantly."[83] However, in light of his admonitions to the community in verses 22–23 Jude's wish that "mercy, peace, and love might increase" becomes tied to Jude's ground of meaning beliefs.

Stassen articulates the essential question for this critical variable: "What do you assume is the channel or vehicle through which goodness becomes effective in the world, *especially in the face of conflict, change, and hope?*"[84] Jude resoundingly answers that the community of faith is the agent or channel of God's mercy.

The Power to do Jude's Ethic

Community participation in the mercy of God is a foundational element in Jude's ground of meaning. Verses 20–23 form the heart Jude's admonition to the community to be faithful and merciful.[85] The power to demonstrate mercy does not come from innate human abilities, rather, Jude outlines three sources which provide the power to do ethics: (1) the power of a community marked by faith (v. 20); (2) the power of the holy spirit appropriated through prayer (v. 20); and (3) the power of a position established by waiting on the mercy of God in Christ (v. 21).

These empowerments correspond to the means of empowerment

articulated by Stassen when he argues that the power to do ethics stems from an understanding of the "...relation between *justification* (forgiveness) and *sanctification* (discipleship)."[86] The community of faith is precisely that group of individuals who by their belief have been justified, and who are now identifiable by their faith.[87] The process of sanctification (discipleship) ideally requires that those who have been justified acknowledge that Jesus Christ is Lord. In Stassen's words:

> The lordship of Christ means that he is Lord in reality and that Christians are called to obey him in the actual situation. Because he *is* Lord, Christians may live with joy and optimism; because he calls people to *serve* him as Lord, Christians may follow him in discipleship, obeying the Holy Spirit and accepting his teachings as norm for their lives.[88]

Jude 20–21 provides a terse statement of the relationship between justification and sanctification. The power to do ethics flows out of the dynamic relationship between the acceptance of forgiveness and the process of discipleship which acknowledges Jesus Christ as Lord.

Jude makes his appeal by calling on the ἀγαπητοί to "be building yourselves up in your holy faith";" be praying in the Holy Spirit;" "keep in the love of God;" "be awaiting the mercy of our Lord Jesus Christ."[89] The "building up in your holy faith" speaks to the power which comes from relating constructively to those individuals whose membership in the community is delineated by their faith.[90] The power to do ethics stems in part from the building up of the community marked by faith. Jude's appeal is not "...that each of his readers should build himself up...but that all should contribute to the spiritual growth of the whole community."[91] The building up in faith is a reminder of the communities justified status, but it is also a prescription for discipleship (sanctification) which demonstrates loyalty and fidelity to the Lord Jesus Christ.[92]

"Praying in the Holy Spirit" is the process of sanctification which appropriates the power of the Spirit by acknowledging the lordship of Christ. Neyrey demonstrates how praying in the Spirit "...could stand for radical freedom (2 Cor 3:17)," but the Spirit can also act "...as the agent of insight into previous statements of Jesus (John 14:26; 15:26; 16:14), and so [support] them."[93] In contrast to the troublemakers in the community—who are without the Spirit, who reject the lordship of Christ (vv. 4, 19)—the faithful acknowledge the lordship of Christ by praying in the Spirit. Neyrey states:

> In this he resembles 1 Cor 12:3, where Paul described true charismatic speech as the affirmation of authority, not freedom: "Jesus is Lord."[94]

Praying in the Spirit is an act of discipleship (sanctification) by which individuals and groups yield to the authority of the Lord Jesus Christ. In turn, the Holy Spirit becomes a source of power to do ethics.

Finally, Jude states the power of position. Neyrey articulates the importance of "keeping" in the correct place as a demonstration of loyalty.[95] The Watchers (v. 6) did not keep themselves in their proper place, and by their actions they were disloyal. The community of faith needs to keep itself in the love of God. In Neyrey's honor/shame configuration: "…the patron [God] has bestowed grace and favor, so the clients [the community of faith] respond with loyalty and faithfulness."[96] Keeping in the love of God demonstrates discipleship (sanctification) which acknowledges Jesus Christ as Lord and appropriates the power to do ethics.

The power of position also relates to the expectant stance of a community of faith which awaits the mercy of our Lord Jesus Christ. Bauckham holds that "'mercy' (ἔλεος) was a traditional term concerning the eschatological hope of God's people."[97] This "waiting for mercy" states the sum of Jude's understanding of the hope of sanctification. The waiting does not "…indicate a merely passive attitude, but an orientation of the whole life toward the eschatological hope."[98] The community of faith waits expectantly the return of the Lord (vv. 14–15) with the hope of being found blameless, and the knowledge that the Lord is the one who can "make you stand blameless before his glory without blemish and in joy" (v. 24).

Verses 20–21, therefore, offer a remarkably compact statement of Jude's understanding of the source of power to do ethics. The power to do ethics—to be the agent of God's mercy in a world of conflict, change, and hope—is generated by the community of faith doing acts of discipleship (sanctification) which acknowledge Jesus' authority as Lord. This in turn allows the community of faith to "…live with joy and optimism" and to "…follow him in discipleship, obeying the Holy Spirit and accepting his teachings as norm for their lives."[99]

Conclusion: Jude's Ground of Meaning

Jude's ground of meaning beliefs are best understood within the context of Jude's apocalyptic worldview. Apocalyptic reckons with how an individual perceives of God's action in and through history (eschatology), and therefore speaks directly to the motivation for ethics. Apocalyptic also deals fundamentally with how individuals should organize community life (ecclesiology), and therefore speaks directly to the content, power, and channel of ethics. The relationship between eschatology and ecclesiology provides the foundation for Jude's ground of meaning beliefs.

Jude's motivation to ethics stems from his understanding of God's action in history both to judge and to save. While Jude's perception of God's saving action in history is not explicit, clearly Jude understands God's action in Jesus Christ as the saving event in history. Jude's articulation of God's judgments within history is explicit, and forms the basis of his argument. The delineation of Old Testament types helps to define and identify the sinful behavior demonstrated by the troublemakers in the community. More important, however, Jude's reference to apocalyptic texts emphasizes that judgment belongs to God, and God alone.

The content, power, and channel of Jude's ethic flow out of this motivation to ethics. The human response to God's action requires moral behavior within the community of faith, but it also demands mercy when there is a breech of that behavior. The channel of God's mercy is the community of faith. The power to do mercy comes from the justified community of faith performing acts of discipleship (sanctification) which acknowledge and yield to the lordship of Christ. The fellowship within the community faith, the power of the Holy Spirit appropriated through prayer, an acute awareness of being kept in the love of God, and the posture of waiting on the mercy of Jesus Christ all empower the community of faith to be the channel or agent of ethical behavior.

Out of these ground of meaning beliefs, it is possible to identify Jude's loyalties, interests, and trusts, his perception of the situation, and finally his mode of moral discourse. Chapter 5 attempts to build on Jude's ground of meaning beliefs in an effort to provide a more integrated analysis of the ethical admonition in the Epistle of Jude.

Chapter Five

Ethical Admonition in the Epistle of Jude

Chapter four argues that Jude's ground of meaning stems primarily from Jude's understanding of the action of God in history and the human response to that action. God continually acts both to judge and to save. Throughout history, God—and God alone—brings judgment upon both groups and individuals who demonstrate ungodly behavior. Yet, Jude also clings to God as savior (vv. 24–25). God through Jesus Christ acts mercifully to bring salvation. The motivation, content, power, and agent of Jude's ethical admonition flow out of the tension between eschatology and ecclesiology.

Jude's concern for eschatology requires an understanding of God's righteous judgments carried to its ultimate conclusion when "the lord comes with his holy myriads to make judgment" (vv. 14–15). Jude's concern for ecclesiology demands an understanding of God's mercy inaugurated in Jesus Christ and acted out by the community of believers (vv. 20–23). These two concerns are the focus of Jude's twofold ethical admonition. While judgment belongs to God alone, mercy is the action of God in Christ in which the community of believers must participate. Both ethical thrusts stem from Jude's ground of meaning beliefs. The final task for a proper understanding of the ethical admonition in the Epistle of Jude is an examination of the text of the letter using the various critical variables which make up the evaluative model. Beginning with the ground of meaning beliefs outlined in chapter four, it is possible to establish Jude's loyalties, interests, and trusts, Jude's perception of the situation, and Jude's mode of moral discourse. The result will be a clearer picture of the ethical admonition in the Epistle of Jude.

Jude's Loyalties, Interests, and Trusts

Four primary loyalties stem from Jude's ground of meaning beliefs and influence Jude's perception of the situation and mode of moral discourse. The first overriding loyalty rises out of Jude's understanding of the content of ethical obligation. God's saving action in Christ and the human response to that action produces a situation in which individuals are kept (τετηρημένοις) and called (κλητοῖς) in Jesus Christ (v. 1). Second, Jude emphasizes the lordship of Jesus Christ, and is ultimately concerned when that authority is denied. Third, Jude displays a remarkable grasp of the certainty of God's righteous judgment exercised on both individuals and groups which have displayed immoral, improper, or unethical behavior. Finally, Jude rests on the mercy of God in Christ as the only hope of standing blameless before the glory of God (vv. 25–25). These elements can be examined under the rubric of Jude's faith dimension, Jude's group loyalties, and Jude's ultimate values.

Jude's Faith Dimension

Jude's emphasis on ἡ ἅπαξ παραδοθείσῃ τοῖς ἁγίοις πίστις (v. 3) and ἡ ἁγιωτάτη ὑμῶν πίστις (v. 20) is best understood as a reminder of the sociological distinctiveness of the community of saints. The human response to God's saving action in Christ creates a new, socially distinct community. Faith is the "badge" or boundary-marker which distinguishes this "kept" and "called" community.

This conception of Jude's understanding of "faith" resonates with N. T. Wright's discussion of Paul's "justification by *belief*, i.e., covenant membership demarcated by that which is believed."[1] Jude, like Paul, is "…anxious about the boundary-markers of the communities he believes himself called upon to found and nurture."[2] Jude, like Paul, has an understanding of "faith" which carries a "sociological cutting edge." To use Wright's conception of faith:

> It is precisely theology, that which is believed, which declares on the one hand that (only) those who *believe* in Christ belong to the community, and on the other that *all* those who believe in Christ, irrespective of racial background, belong.[3]

The "faith once delivered to the saints" (τῇ ἅπαξ παραδοθείσῃ τοῖς ἁγίοις πίστει, v. 3) is the distinctive criterion which sets apart the "kept" and "called" community.[4] It is the foundation upon which the community can be built (ἐποικοδομοῦντες ἑαυτοὺς τῇ ἁγιωτάτῃ ὑμῶν πίστει, v. 21).

Jude's Group Loyalties

Jude demonstrates tremendous loyalty to this kept, and called community of faith. Jude reveals his love, and compassion for the community of faith in his reference to them as ἀγαπητοί (vv. 3, 17, 20). Jude displays gentle, respectful restraint when reminding the community of what they should already know (῾Υπομνῆσαι δὲ ὑμᾶς βούλομαι, εἰδότας [ὑμᾶς] πάντα, v. 5; ῾Υμεῖς δέ, ἀγαπητοί, μνήσθητε τῶν ῥημάτων τῶν προειρημένων ὑπὸ τῶν ἀποστόλων τοῦ κυρίου ἡμῶν ᾿Ιησοῦ Χριστοῦ, v. 17). Moreover, the occasion for Jude's writing stems from his concern for the integrity of the group (παρεισέδυσαν γάρ τινες ἄνθρωποι, v. 4). In addition, Jude's comparison of the troublemakers (οὗτοι, vv. 8, 10, 12, 16, 19) with the faithful drives the argument of the letter and demonstrates Jude's concern for the community of faith.

Jude's Ultimate Values

Jude's ultimate values grow naturally out of his ground of meaning beliefs. While several themes or concepts might be identified, three ultimate values suggest themselves: (1) the lordship of Jesus Christ; (2) the certainty of God's judgment; and (3) the importance of mercy.

The Lordship of Jesus Christ. The text of Jude reveals much about the development of Christology in the early Christian community.[5] Jude's twenty-five verses are replete with expressions and titles which emphasize the lordship of Jesus Christ. Jesus is "the Christ" (ὁ Χριστός, vv. 1, 4, 17, 21, 25); "the Lord" (ὁ κύριος, vv. 5 [possibly], 14); "our Lord" (ὁ κυρίος ὑμῶν, vv. 4, 17, 21, 25); and "master" (ὁ δεσπότης, v. 4).[6]

Jude writes as a "slave of Jesus Christ" (v. 1), and he refers to "the apostles of our Lord Jesus Christ" (v. 17). Moreover, it is "Jesus Christ our Lord" who effects God's salvation in the world (v. 25), and it is the Lord who "comes with holy myriads to make judgment" (v. 14–15). Jude admonishes demonstrations of allegiance to the lordship of Jesus Christ (vv. 20–21), and he warns the community about those who would deny the lordship of Jesus Christ (v. 4).[7]

The Certainty of Judgment. Jude's understanding of the certainty of God's judgment stems directly from his ground of meaning beliefs. Jude values this understanding of God's action in history, and it holds a prominent place in the argument of the letter. The motivation to ethics stems from an understanding of the certainty of judgment. Those who demonstrate immoral or unethical behavior need to be aware of the certainty of God's judgment on the wicked. Jude's perception of God's action in history demonstrates that judgment is certain; however, Jude does not simply hold out the threat of punishment as an extrinsic motivation to correct behavior. Jude is more concerned to establish the certainty of God's judgment as a motivation for acts of mercy within the community of faith.

Jude values the certainty of judgment because it places judgment in the hands of God and takes it away from the hands of the community of faith. When the community of faith understands and values the certainty of God's judgment against the wicked, it is freed to do acts of discipleship (vv. 20–21) which yield the power to do acts of mercy (vv. 22–23).

The Importance of Mercy. While Jude's articulation of the certainty of judgment is often the sole emphasis of many commentators, the unique position of mercy in Jude's argument is often overlooked. Jude wishes an abundance of mercy for his readers (v. 2). The community of faith is to await mercy (v. 21). Jude admonishes the community of faith to demonstrate mercy on the sinful (vv. 22–23). In the end, Jude describes the merciful act of God through Jesus Christ as the only reason the faithful can keep from falling, "and stand blameless before his glory in great joy" (vv. 24–25). Jude opens with a wish for mercy, admonishes the community to demonstrate mercy, and reminds the community that their position before God is the result of mercy.

Jude's emphasis on mercy resonates with James 2:13 ("for judgment without mercy will be shown to anyone who has not been merciful; Mercy triumphs over judgment!" [NIV]), and it stands in line with Jesus' emphasis in the Sermon on the Mount ("Blessed are the merciful, for they will be shown mercy," Matt 5:7 [NIV]). While James admonition to show mercy maintains a negative thrust, and the words of Jesus as recorded in Matthew hold a positive thrust, Jude's admonitions are sober and thoughtful. James promises judgment if mercy is not shown. Jesus assures mercy if mercy is shown. Jude admonishes mercy, but he acknowledges the difficulties and dangers of being merciful to the most sinful (v. 23, οὓς δὲ ἐλεᾶτε ἐν φόβῳ).

Jude's ultimate values, like his group loyalties and his understanding of faith, stem from his ground of meaning beliefs. The lordship of Christ, the certainty of judgment, and the importance of mercy is verifiable in the perception of God's actions in and through history. A challenge to these ultimate values provides the occasion for Jude's writing and can be described as Jude's perception of the situation.

Jude's Perception of the Situation

The perception of the situation relates primarily to Jude's perception of the threat facing the community of faith, Jude's understanding of authority, and Jude's articulation of the means of change within the community. Again, these variables are closely related to Jude's ground of meaning beliefs, and they relate specifically to Jude's loyalties, interests, and trusts.

The threat Jude perceives is twofold. First, and most prominent in the text, is the threat of incorrect behavior among those who count themselves as part of the community of faith. Second, and perhaps more significant for a fresh understanding of the ethical admonition in Jude, is the threat of an unmerciful spirit among those who count themselves as part of the community of faith. These two threats combine to form the basis for Jude's occasion to write. The degree of the threat appears significant in that Jude moves from writing a letter "concerning our common salvation," and feels compelled to write "encouraging you to contend for the faith once given to the saints" (v. 3). The threats are linked to each other in that the unmerciful spirit is directed precisely against those individuals who are demonstrating incorrect behavior. Moreover, both threats stem from the inability to fully acknowledge the lordship of Christ.

Incorrect Behavior in the Community of Faith

In Jude's perception of the situation, the "secret entry of certain persons" (v. 4, παρεισέδυσαν γάρ τινες ἄνθρωποι) is the precipitating event which establishes the twofold threat to the community of faith. These individuals hold themselves out to be members of the community of faith, claiming to bear the faith which has become the social distinctive for the community.

Moreover, these individuals are fully integrated into the life of the community of faith. They eat at the community meals (v. 12, οὗτοι εἰσιν οἱ ἐν ταῖς ἀγάπαις ὑμων), and they have the power and position to cause disputes within the community (v. 19). This identification of the troublemakers as integrated members of the community of faith is vital for a proper understanding of the ethical admonition in the Epistle of Jude. While the problems faced by Jude may have originated outside the community of faith, they are now fully entrenched within the community.

These individuals deny the lordship of Jesus Christ, a direct contradiction to the ultimate value that Jude places on this principle. They "deny the only master and our Lord Jesus Christ" (v. 4, τὸν μόνον δεσπότην καὶ κύριον ἡμῶν Ἰησοῦν Χριστὸν ἀρνούμενοι). They "reject authority" (v. 8, κυριότητα δὲ ἀθετοῦσιν) and "blaspheme the glory" (v. 8, δόξας δὲ βλασφημοῦσιν).[8] In addition, these individuals "go after their own desires," (v. 16, κατὰ τὰς ἐπιθυμίας ἑαυτῶν πορευόμενοι). In this, they fit the pattern predicted by the apostles: "In the last time there will be scoffers following after their own ungodly desires," (v. 18, κατὰ τὰς ἑαυτῶν ἐπιθυμίας πορευόμενοι τῶν ἀσεβειῶν).

In contrast to the sanctifying acts of discipleship urged by Jude that demonstrate allegiance to the lordship of Jesus Christ, these individuals flout authority and live by instinct (vv. 8, 10, 19). They do not build up the community of faith. Rather, they "ridicule things they don't understand" (v. 10, οὗτοι δὲ ὅσα μὲν οὐκ οἴδασιν βλασφημοῦσιν) and cause disputes (v. 19, Οὗτοί εἰσιν οἱ ἀποδιοριζοντες). They are the "grumblers" and "faultfinders" (v. 16, γογγυσταὶ μεμψίμοιροι). They "shepherd themselves" (v. 12, ἑαυτοὺς ποιμαίνοντες) rather than the whole community. Their speech does not build up the community of faith, but rather "their mouths speak highly and they flatter others for the sake of advantage" (v. 16, καὶ τὸ στόμα αὐτων λαλεῖ ὑπέρογκα, θαυμάζοντες πρόσωπα ὠφελείας χάριν).

In contrast to Jude's admonition to "pray in the Spirit," these individuals "do not have the Spirit" (v. 19, πνεῦμα μὴ ἔχοντες). Praying in the Spirit demonstrates an allegiance to the lordship of Jesus Christ. Those who deny the lordship of Jesus Christ don't even have the Spirit. They are like "wild animals" (v. 10, ὡς τὰ ἄλογα ζῷα) following their own instincts (v. 10, ὅσα δὲ φυσικῶς, v. 19, ψυχικοί). The absence of the Spirit leaves them as:

clouds without rain, blown along by the wind; fruitless harvest trees, twice dead, uprooted; wild waves of the sea foaming up their own ungodliness; wandering planets to which the gloom of darkness has been kept for ever (vv. 12–13).

Their denial of the lordship of Jesus Christ runs counter to their claim to be part of the community of faith. Moreover, their denials of Christ's authority are accentuated by acts of immoral behavior. These individuals "pervert the grace of our God into vice," (v. 4, τὴν τοῦ θεοῦ ἡμῶν χάριτα μετατιθέντες εἰς ἀσέλγειαν) and "pollute the flesh" (v. 8, σάρκα μὲν μιαίνουσιν). In contrast to the behavior that Jude admonishes—acts of discipleship which demonstrate allegiance to the lordship of Christ—the troublemakers' behavior denies the authority of Christ.

The presence of these individuals within the community of faith presents Jude a significant challenge. If Jude has a specific heresy in mind, there is little evidence with which to make such a judgment. If no specific heresy can be identified, what can be said with certainty? Jude's concern for proper ethical behavior within the community of faith is paramount.[9] The infiltration of these "certain individuals" has led to an untenable situation within the community of faith. Individuals who claim to be members of the community are committing immoral acts and possibly influencing others. Their rejection of the lordship of Christ is clear. Their presence, however, has caused another type of rebellion to demonstrate itself within the community of faith.

An Unmerciful Spirit in the Community of Faith

Rejection of the lordship of Jesus Christ manifests itself in many ways. The obvious demonstrations of ungodliness deserve the strong rebuke afforded them by Jude. Less obvious perhaps, but no less important for our understanding of the ethical admonition in the Epistle of Jude is the denial of the lordship of Jesus Christ which demonstrates itself by an unmerciful spirit.

Jude's concern for demonstrations of mercy dominates the admonition in verses 22–23. Jude admonishes mercy and acts of mercy on even the most sinful. Jude admonishes mercy to the "doubters" (disputers, v. 22, διακρινομένους). Those that are already in the fire are to be saved (v. 23, οὓς δὲ σώζετε ἐκ πυρὸς ἁπάζοντες). Even those whose sin should be feared and avoided are to be shown mercy (v. 23, οὓς δὲ ἐλεᾶτε ἐν φόβῳ μισοῦντες καὶ τὸν ἀπὸ τῆς σαρκὸς ἐσπιλωμένον χιτῶνα). Jude's instruction to the community of faith to demonstrate mercy toward even the most sinful flows directly from his ground of meaning beliefs: Judgment belongs to God alone; mercy is the act of God in Christ in which the community of faith can and must participate.[10]

Jude's ultimate values—the lordship of Christ, the certainty of judgment, and the importance of mercy—define the parameters of Jude's perception of the situation. The lordship of Christ is denied by those members of the community of faith who demonstrate immoral, unethical, and incorrect behavior. Their judgment is certain, but it is the judgment of God not the community of faith. Conversely, the lordship of Christ is denied by those members of the community of faith who fail to understand the importance of mercy.

Jude's Mode of Moral Discourse: Contextualist

Jude makes his argument by operating at the level of basic beliefs. Jude responds to a new ethical dilemma by applying his basic beliefs to the perceived problems. By this, Jude demonstrates the characteristics of a contextualist. The contextualist's response to an ethical dilemma is not generated by adherence to a rule, or a principle; but rather, the contextualist responds out of ground of meaning beliefs.

Jude's ground of meaning beliefs are generated by the perception of God's action in history and the human response to God's action. Judgment is certain, but it belongs to God alone. Mercy can and must be demonstrated by the community of faith. Jude's mode of moral discourse applies these basic beliefs to a situation in which the lordship of Christ is denied both through demonstrations of incorrect behavior and an unmerciful spirit in the community of faith.

Jude brings considerable exegetical and rhetorical strength to the argument presented in the letter.[11] Jude's skillful use of OT types and creative citation of apocalyptic texts is evident; however, the foundational nature of the ground of meaning beliefs which drive his contextualist answer to the perceived problem must not be subsumed to the literary means of presentation. Jude's contextualist answer to the problem created by the presence of incorrect behavior within the community of faith is the simple application of basic beliefs to an ethical dilemma. In this, Jude "...speaks profoundly to the human situation from the richness and depth of Christian Faith."[12]

Conclusion

The ethical admonition in the Epistle of Jude deserves a renewed emphasis within the community of faith. Jude's twofold admonition stems from deeply held ground of meaning beliefs which are demonstrated in Jude's apocalyptic worldview. Jude understands God's action throughout history to judge, and he holds that out as the motivation to ethics. Jude also understands God's action in Jesus Christ to save. By this saving action, a new community is created. A community marked by faith which yields allegiance to the lordship of Christ.

Those who claim membership in this community are responsible to demonstrate correct behavior. When this responsibility is breached God's judgment is certain, but it remains God's judgment. Allegiance to the lordship of Christ requires that the community of faith demonstrate mercy to even the worst sinners. The power to be the agent of God's mercy stems not from human ability, but from acts of discipleship (sanctification) which demonstrate a yielding to the lordship of Christ.

When seen in this light, Jude is far more than "mere denunciation" or "violent polemic." Jude stands as a strong admonition to the community of faith to demonstrate allegiance to the lordship of Jesus Christ both by correct behavior and by acts of mercy. The contention that the admonition in the Epistle of Jude is too time and situation specific to be of value for the modern community of faith must be reevaluated.[13] The church needs a reminder of the certainty of God's judgment; but it also needs to understand its function as the agent of God's mercy.

This study demonstrates the remarkable unity of purpose and message that is the New Testament. Jude stands shoulder to shoulder with the ethical admonition of James (Jam 2:12) and Jesus (Matt 5:7). Jude's understanding of "faith" as the marker of the new community compares with Paul's concern for justification by belief in which "faith" carries a sociological significance. To some extent, therefore, the preceding study lends support to the presuppositional thesis that Jude represents theological reflection within the early community of faith about the relationship between eschatology (God's action in and through history) and ecclesiology (the human response to God's action in the living of everyday life).

Application of the evaluative model to other texts in the New Testament should reveal similar ground of meaning beliefs and ultimate values. A study of Jesus discourse in Mark 13, or the parables in Matt 25 might demonstrate lines of connection between the ethical admonition in Jude and the sayings of Jesus. In addition, one suspects that the application of the model to the ethical mandates of Paul (e.g., 1 Cor 5), or the paraenetic instruction in James would yield a wealth of information about how ground of meaning beliefs influence the perception of the situation, and the mode of moral discourse respectively.

Finally, Jude's articulation of the importance of correct behavior within the community of faith cannot be overemphasized. The claim to hold and defend the "faith once for all delivered to the saints" is only legitimate when it is validated by a yielding to the lordship of Jesus Christ. This yielding certainly involves taking seriously Jude's admonition to demonstrate correct behavior within the community of faith; but perhaps more importantly, demands that the community of faith take seriously its role as the agent of God's mercy.

Notes

Notes for Chapter One

1. Douglas J. Rowston, "The Most Neglected Book in the New Testament," *New Testament Studies*, 21 (1974–75): 554–563. The title of Rowston's article seems more often cited than the actual substance of his research. Rowston's earlier and less celebrated work "The Setting of the Letter of Jude" (Th.D. diss., The Southern Baptist Theological Seminary, 1971) stands as the lone attempt at the Southern Baptist Theological Seminary to offer attention to the Epistle of Jude in the last twenty–five years!

2. Roman Heiligenthal, *Zwischen Henoch und Paulus: Studien zum theologiegeschichtlichen Ort des Judasbriefes*, TANZ 6 (Tübingen: Franke, 1992): 1, links this *Schattendasein* to the "heritage of reformation exegesis" which saw Jude as derived from 2 Peter and void of any preaching of Christ—a conclusion which Heiligenthal argues was "reached not exegetically, but dogmatically."

3. J.Daryl Charles, *Literary Strategy in the Epistle of Jude* (Scranton: University of Scranton Press, 1993), 15.

4. Witness primarily Richard Bauckham, *Jude, 2 Peter*, Word Biblical Commentary, vol. 50 (Waco: Word Books, 1983); *Jude and the Relatives of Jesus in the Early Church* (Edinburgh: T & T Clark, 1990); J. Daryl Charles, *Literary Strategy in the Epistle of Jude*; Roman Heiligenthal, *Zwischen Henoch und Paulus*; Jerome H. Neyrey, *2 Peter, Jude*, The Anchor Bible, vol. 37c (New York: Doubleday, 1993); Henning Paulsen, *Der Zweite Petrusbrief und der Judasbrief*. Kritisch-exegetischer Kommentar uber das Neue Testament, XII/2 (Gottingen: Vanderhoeck & Ruprecht, 1992); Anton Vögtle, *Der Judasbrief, Der Zweite Petrusbrief*, Evangelisch-Katholischer Kommentar zum Neuen Testament, 22 (Düsseldorff: Benzinger Verlag; Neukirchen-Vluyn: Neukircher Verlag, 1994).

5. Recent treatments of the Epistle of Jude have given more attention to the role of the letter in the developing teaching and theology of the early Christian community. In *Jude and the Relatives of Jesus in the Early Church*, Bauckham cogently argues the significance of Jude for our understanding of the early Christian communities developing Christology. Rowston, "The Setting of the Letter of Jude," argues less convincingly the position of Jude as a corrective to misunderstood Pauline theology, placing the letter on a continuum of theological thought beginning with Paul and ending with 2 Peter.

6. On the rhetoric of Jude see Duane F. Watson, *Invention, Arrangement, and Style: Rhetorical Criticism of Jude and 2 Peter* (Atlanta: Scholars Press, 1988); on literary analysis, J. Daryl Charles, *Literary Strategy in the Epistle of Jude*; on the historical setting, Roman Heiligenthal, *Zwischen Henoch und Paulus*. Heiligenthal proposes a *theologiegeschichtlichen* location for the Epistle of Jude which is similar to Rowston's identification of Jude as a

corrective to misunderstood Pauline theology. Heiligenthal goes further by relating Jude specifically to the "heresy" faced by the community addressed in Colossians. On the sociological analysis of Jude see Jerome Neyrey, *Jude, 2 Peter.*

7. Bauckham argues convincingly that "among those who played a creative theological role in the crucially important earliest decades of Christianity were the relatives of Jesus." *Jude and the Relatives of Jesus in the Early Church*, 3. In context, the Epistle of Jude stands as a statement on how theology should determine behavior.

8. This concern is articulated by Neyrey in his discussion of the authenticity of Jude: "Arguments for and against authenticity, moreover, tend to depend on scholarly assessments of the dating of the document and its contents," *2 Peter, Jude*, 31. See also Donald Guthrie, *New Testament Introduction* (Downers Grove: Intervarsity Press, 1970), 922. In a discussion of the different views of J. W. C. Wand, and Charles Bigg, Guthrie states: "Obviously both approach the data having already made up their minds in which direction the dependence lies and both have reasonable arguments in support"(ibid.).

9. Vögtle, *Der Judasbrief*, 12: "Das verrät schon der Umstand, dass sich zahlreiche Autoren über diesen Punkt ausschweigen oder auch annähernd allen Vorschlägen Rechnung getragen wird: Judas könnte '...sich in besonderer Weise nach dem Tod des Jakobus für die Judenchristen in Palästina, Syrien, Ägypten zuständig gefühlt haben, wobei sein Einfluss bis zu den Judenchristen in Kleinasien und in Rom reichte.'" Vögtle cites O. Knoch, *Der erste und zweite Petrusbrief. Der Judasbrief*, Regensbuger Neues Testament (1990), 161.

10. Bauckham, *Jude, 2 Peter*, 8. The majority of treatments of Jude and 2 Peter are catalogued as treatments of "the General Epistles," or "the Catholic Epistles." See also, *Jude and the Relatives of Jesus*, 155ff.

11. Certainly Bauckham has helped to remove the stigma of "early Catholic" from our perception of the Epistle of Jude; however, it is the contention of this study that not enough has been done to place emphasis on the primary message of the letter, namely ethical admonition!

12. See Rowston, "The Setting of the Letter of Jude."

13. Here I am indebted to Christopher L. Church, "A *Forschungsgeschichte* on the Literary Character of the Epistle of James" (Ph.D. diss., The Southern Baptist Theological Seminary, 1990), 9. Church demonstrates that dissertations do not have to be "methodologically driven" in order to be effective.

14. Glen Stassen, "Critical Variables in Christian Social Ethics," in *Issues in Christian Ethics*, ed. Paul D. Simmons (Nashville: Broadman Press, 1980). Cf. Stassen, "A Social Theory Model for Religious Social Ethics," *Journal of Religious Ethics* (Spring 1977): 9–37.

15. Christopher Rowland, *The Open Heaven: A Study of Apocalyptic in Judaism and Early Christianity* (London: SPCK, 1982).

16. For a review of scholarship on critical issues see Richard J. Bauckham, "The Letter of Jude: An Account of Research," *ANRW* 2/25/5, ed. W. Hasse (Berlin/New York: de Gruyter, 1988), 3791–3826. This article is expanded and revised in Bauckham's *Jude and the Relatives of Jesus in the Early Church* (Edinburgh: T & T Clark, 1990), 134–178. See also Roman Heiligenthal, "Der Judasbrief: Aspekte der Forschung in den letzten Jahrzehnten," *Theologische Rundschau* 51 (1986): 117–129.

17. For example, D.F. Watson, *Invention, Arrangement, and Style*, provides a cogent rhetorical analysis of both Jude and 2 Peter, but concludes his study by dealing with questions of literary dependence between the two letters, 147–189.

18. See J. J. Gunther, "The Alexandrian Epistle of Jude," *New Testament Studies* 30 (1984): 549–62. Gunther revives the Alexandrian Hypothesis for the origin of the Epistle of Jude, which he states was first proposed by Ernst Th. Mayerhoff in *Historisch-kritische Einleitung in die petrinischen Schriften* (Hamburg: Perthes, 1835), 195. See Otto Pfleiderer, *Primitive Christianity: Its Writings and Teachings in Their Historical Connections*, vol. 4, trans. W. Montgomery (Clifton, NJ: Reference Book Publishers, 1965). To his credit, Gunther relies more on internal evidence as over against Pfleiderer who assumes a second century dating based on his understanding of Jude's opponents as Carpocratian Gnostics, and then speculates an Alexandrian origin for the letter.

19. Vögtle, *Der Judasbrief*, 114: "Das argumentationsverfahren unseres Briefes ist derart zeit- und situationsbedingt, dass das Gros seiner Textstücke für die gottesdienstliche Lesung völlig ungeeignet ist."

20. The "early catholic" designation is by far the more predominant. See for example, Thomas Barns, "The Epistle of St. Jude in the Marcosian Heresy," *Journal of Theological Studies* 6 (1905):391–411; George R. Beasley-Murray, *The General Epistles* (New York: Abingdon Press, 1965); J. C. Beker, "Jude, Epistle of," *IDB*, vol. 2, ed. G. A. Buttrick (New York: Abingdon Press, 1962):1009–1011; Gerhard Krodel, "The Epistle of Jude," *Proclamation Commentaries* (Philadelphia: Fortress Press, 1977); Norman Perrin, *The New Testament: An Introduction* (New York: Harcourt, Brace, Jovanovich Inc., 1974); Bo Reicke, *Epistles of James, Peter and Jude*, Anchor Bible, vol. 37 (Garden City: Doubleday, 1982); Theodor Zahn, *Introduction to the New Testament*, trans. Melancton W. Jacobus (New York: Charles Scribner's Sons, 1917). The classification "early Catholic" refers to the development of the early forms of the Catholic church and should be distinguished from the term "catholic," which refers to a universal letter addressed to the churches at large.

21. Fewer scholars can be placed in this classification. See for example E. Earle Ellis, *Prophecy and Hermeneutic in Early Christianity* (Tübingen: J. C. B. Mohr, 1978); Douglas Rowston, "The Setting of the Letter of Jude"; Richard Bauckham, *Jude, 2 Peter*. A more thorough

discussion of the positions of recent interpretations is found in chapter three.

22. Ernst Käsemann, "An Apologia For Primitive Christian Eschatology," *Essays on New Testament Themes*, Studies in Biblical Theology, no. 41 (Chatham: SCM Press, 1964), 169–195. The article originated as a series of lectures given in late 1952 and was first published in *Zeitschrift für Theologie und Kirche* 49 (1952): 272–296.

23. Heiligenthal, "Der Judasbrief," 121: "Mit dieser theologischen Einordnung und Wertung des Jude bestimmte K. die Richtung eines Grossteils der protestantischen Forschung nach ihm."

24. The continuing dominance of the "early Catholic" designation among even Baptist scholars is seen in the brief discussion of Jude and 2 Peter by Marty Reid, "Images of the Church in the General Epistles," in *The People of God: Essays on the Believers' Church*, ed. Paul Basden and David Dockery (Nashville: Broadman Press, 1991), 173.

25. Bauckham, *Jude, 2 Peter*, 8ff. Bauckham attributes these criteria to J. D. G. Dunn, *Unity and Diversity in the New Testament* (London: SCM Press, 1977).

26. Bauckham, *Jude and the Relatives of Jesus*, 160. Cf. Michael Desjardins, "The Portrayal of the Dissidents in 2 Peter and Jude: Does it tell us more about the 'Godly' than the 'Ungodly'?," *Journal for the Study of the New Testament* 30 (1987): 91–93. Desjardins suggests that "δόξας δὲ βλασφημιαίνουσιν" (v. 8) refers to rebellion against church officials. Bauckham points out that Desjardins makes this assertion without any supporting evidence.

27. Vögtle, *Der Judasbrief*, 3: "Als Hohepunkt greift er zur christologisch interpretierten Endgerichtsprophetie von athHen 1,9…, um den Glauben an den mit einer Engeleskorte zum Bericht kommenden- und die Gegner ihrer Tatund Wortsünden überführenden- Christus auch positive zu begrunden (v. 14–16)." At almost no point does Vögtle agree with Bauckham's conclusions. Here, however, he seems to confirm Bauckham's assertion that there is no loss of the Parousia hope seen in the letter.

28. Bauckham, *Jude and the Relatives of Jesus*, cites J. N. D. Kelly, *A Commentary on The Epistles of Peter and Jude* (New York: Harper & Row, 1969), 248. Jude's use of "the faith" suggests "…a formalized view of the Church's message as a clearly defined and authoritatively transmitted deposit…." Bauckham points out that "this interpretation of Jude's view of faith and tradition recurs throughout the literature on Jude from the nineteenth century to the present day" (158).

29. Bauckham, *Jude, 2 Peter*, 9.

30. Ibid. The popular stigma of "mere denunciation" in modern scholarship may be traced to the classic commentary by J. B. Mayor, *The Epistle of St. Jude and the Second Epistle of St. Peter* (London: Macmillan, 1907). In making a distinction from 2 Peter, Mayor argues that "…Jude is throughout occupied with the denunciation of evil-doers…"(xvi). This

characterization of Jude's argument as mere denunciation has held sway through the twentieth century. Cf. Adolf Jülicher, *An Introduction to the New Testament*, trans. Janet Penrose Ward (London: Smith, Elder, & Co., 1904); J. W. C. Wand, *The General Epistles of St. Peter and St. Jude* (London: Methuen and Co., 1934); James Moffatt, *The General Epistles: James, Peter, Judas* (London: Hodder and Stoughton, 1928); Werner G. Kummel, *Introduction to the New Testament*, trans. Howard Clark Kee (Nashville: Abingdon Press, 1975); and Gerhard Krodel, *The Epistle of Jude* (Philadelphia: Fortress Press, 1977).

31. Pfleiderer, *Primitive Christianity*, 251.

32. Beasley-Murray, *The General Epistles*, 72.

33. Kelly, *A Commentary*, 288.

34. Eric Fuchs and Pierre Reymond, *La Deuxieme Épître de Saint Pierre, L'Épître de Saint Jude*, Commentaire du Nouveau Testament, second series 13b (Paris: Delachaux & Niestle, 1980), 141.

35. Gunther, "The Alexandrian Epistle," 554.

36. Karl Herman Schelkle, *Die Petrusbriefe, Der Judasbrief*, Herders Theologischer Kommentar zum Neuen Testament, 13/2, ed. Alfred Wikenhyauser and Anton Vögtle (Freiburg/Basel/Wien: Herder, 1961), 137.

37. Kümmel, *Introduction*, states: "It is significant that the views of the Gnostics are not really answered in detail; rather the false teachers are scolded and threatened with God's judgment....This mode of polemic against heretics runs counter to the combating of false teachers elsewhere in the NT, but that is in keeping with the fact that the letter does not contain any real message of Christ at all, and with its 'early Catholic' concept of faith stands in unrelieved tension with the understanding of faith in the chief witnesses of the NT" (426).

38. Bauckham, *Jude and the Relatives of Jesus*, 156. Bauckham follows E. Earle Ellis, *Prophecy and Hermeneutic*, and suggests that "the polemical section (vv. 4–19) is not in fact 'mere denunciation' but...is carefully composed pesher exegesis..." (157).

39. Ibid., 152–154. See also *Jude, 2 Peter*, 4.

40. Ibid., 161. Bauckham points out that "...the apocalyptic features of [Jude's] thought and background are too obvious to be missed even by scholars who stress its 'early Catholic' character."

41. Rowston, "The Setting of the Letter of Jude."

42. Vögtle, *Der Judasbrief*, 7: "Angesichts dieser Identifizierung der Gegner kann es nicht überraschen, dass Bauckham nach wie vor betont, der Streit gehe nicht um 'Orthadoxie und Häresie im Glauben, sondern um die beziehung zwischen Evangelium und moralischer Verpflichtung' um 'die moralischen Implikation des Evangeliums.'"

43. For a list of proposed dates from A.D. 54, Renan (1869) to A.D. 160, Barns (1905), see Bauckham, *Jude and the Relatives of Jesus*, 168–69.

44. Guthrie, *Introduction*, 908.

45. Wand, *The General Epistles*, 190. Wand outlines the prevailing views of earlier scholarship as follows: (1) the Tübingen School which posited a late 2nd century date revealing a Jewish-Christian reaction against Pauline theology; (2) the views of Otto Pfleiderer, who suggested that the letter was directed against Carpocratian Gnostics and dated at approximately A.D. 150; and (3) Adolf Harnack, who saw the letter as directed against Syrian Gnostics and dated it at around A.D. 100–130. See also Fuchs and Reymond, *La Deuxieme Épître de Saint Pierre, L'Épître de Saint Jude*, 151 n. 1.

46. Michael Knibb, *The Ethiopic Book of Enoch: A New Edition in the Light of the Aramaic Dead Sea Fragments*, 2 vols. (Oxford: Clarendon Press, 1978).

47. Johannes Tromp, *The Assumption of Moses: A Critical Edition with Commentary*, Studia In Veteris Testamenti Pseudepigrapha, ed. A. M. Denis and M. DeJonge, 10 (Leiden: E. J. Brill, 1993): 116.

48. C. E. B. Cranfield, *I and II Peter, and Jude*, (London: SCM Press, 1960), 147.

49. A. R. C. Leaney, *The Letters of Peter and Jude* (Cambridge: Cambridge University Press, 1967), 82.

50. Zahn, *Introduction*, 241, who characterizes "faith" as "…the unalterable summary of religious convictions and teachings which has been communicated once and for all to the church," but in an effort to maintain the genuine authorship and priority of 2 Peter argues for a rather early date of A.D. 75.

51. Positions on how v. 17 affects the issue of dating range from arguments for an early date because the verse implies that the audience knew and heard the apostles directly (Bauckham, *Jude, 2 Peter*, 12; F. H. Chase, "Jude, Epistle of," *Dictionary of the Bible*, ed. James Hastings, vol. 2 [New York: Charles Schribner's Sons, 1902]: 799–800; Cranfield, *Jude*, 146]) to the position that v. 17 definitely implies "long retrospect," and the passing of the Apostolic Age (Beasley-Murray, *The General Epistles*, 73; Beker, "Jude", 1010; Fuchs and Reymond, *L'Épître de Saint Jude*, 151; Mayor, *The Epistle of St. Jude*, cxiv; Schelkle, *Der Judasbrief*, 138; Vögtle, *Der Judasbrief*, 8).

52. George R. Beasley-Murray's assertion in *The General Epistles* that Jude "…must be set after the death of the apostles (verse 17), late enough for Gnostics to have become active in the churches,…and probably long enough after the fall of Jerusalem for it no longer to dominate the horizon of Jewish Christianity" (73–74) is so filled with tentative suppositions, that the removal of any one of them causes his position to collapse. Because he believes v. 17 to be a reference to the death of apostles, it must be after the fall of Jerusalem, but because the fall of Jerusalem is not hinted at in Jude it must have been written a long time after the fall, but because of his concern to make Jude the genuine author he is forced to wedge the letter into a very small time frame—A.D. 80!

53. E. M. Sidebottom, *James, Jude, and 2 Peter*, New Century Bible (London: Thomas Nelson and Sons, 1967), 75. Sidebottom acknowledges additional similarities with *1 Clement* 20:12, *Herm. Sim.* 5:7:2, *Did.* 2:7, but concludes "whatever affinities there are between Jude and the Apostolic Fathers are explainable on the grounds of similar use of language, and not of borrowing." Sidebottom's A.D. 120 dating requires some explanation of such similarities which would not allow for Jude being "borrowed" before the second century.

54. Bauckham, *Jude, 2 Peter*, 21–23. Bauckham provides an excellent review of the evidence for and against each of the choices.

55. Ibid., 21–22. Bauckham cites John Calvin and Matthew Henry as examples of "older commentators" who have made this identification.

56. Cf. Gunther, "The Alexandrian Epistle," 557, who favors a late date around A.D. 120–130 and proposes that the author was possibly the Bishop of Alexandria.

57. Ellis, 226ff. Ellis discusses the meaning of the phrase οἱ ἀδελφοί, and its importance for our understanding of the identification of the author of Jude. Ellis favors a date between 55–65.

58. Heiligenthal, "Der Judasbrief," 120: "The pseudepigraphal character of Jude is contested no more." Heiligenthal seems to be unaware of the significant contribution of Bauckham to this discussion.

59. Barns, 391 (A.D. 160); Kummel, 429 (turn of the century); Leaney, 82 (A.D. 100); Reicke, 192 (A.D. 90); Schelkle, 138 (A.D. 90); and Sidebottom, 78 (A.D. 120). In support of a late date, and pseudepigraphal authorship of the letter, commentators cite the account of Eusebius, *History of the Church* 3:19–20:8, who recalls Hegesippus' story of the grandsons of Jude appearing before the emperor Domitian. Bauckham, *Jude, 2 Peter*, refutes this "uncritical" treatment of the account and suggests that the story need not support an author other than Jude (15).

60. Bauckham, *Jude, 2 Peter*, 15. Bauckham makes this simple yet incisive observation in response to the critical gymnastics engaged in by some scholars. Cf. Sidebottom, *Jude*, 78–79, who touts the presumed significance of the individual Jude/Didymus/Thomas to the Gnostics

and argues for a pseudonymous authorship intended to combat gnostics at a point of their own celebration, namely the claim that Jude was the "twin" of Jesus.

61. Vögtle, *Der Judasbrief*, 11: "Weil er aber um den längst erfolgten Tod des Jakobus wusste, wählte er als Pseudonym 'Judas', der Jakobus überlebt haben muss und dessen Name gegen Ende des 1. Jh. jedenfalls noch bekannt war, und fügte in der intitulatio 'Bruder des Jakobus' hinzu, um Judas von anderen Trägen dieses Namens zu unterscheiden und zugleich seine Legitimation für seinen Lehranspruch zu unterstreichen (s.zu. v.1)."

62. Bauckham, *Jude, 2 Peter*, 14, argues that if the letter is pseudepigraphal and comes from a Palestinian Jewish-Christian context, "…it is inexplicable that the letter does not call Jude 'the brother of the Lord,' the title by which he was always known in such circles and which his authority was indicated. The description of Jude as 'brother of James' only (v.1) is much more easily explicable on the hypothesis of authenticity than on that of pseudepigraphy."

63. Ibid., 15.

64. Most notable is Martin Hengel, *Judaism and Hellenism*, 2 vols. (Minneapolis: Fortress Press, 1974). Cf. Louis Feldman, "Hengel's Judaism and Hellenism In Retrospect," *Journal of Biblical Literature* 96 (Spring 1977): 371–382. J. A. T. Robinson states, "it is clear…that both [the opponents] and the writer and presumably those to whom he is writing belong to a dominantly, if not exclusively, Jewish-Christian milieu within the Hellenistic world." *Redating the New Testament* (London: SCM Press, 1976), 170–171. Recent reflection on the influence of Hellenistic culture on all of the 1st century world makes assertions like Robinson's seem imprecise at best.

65. Bauckham, *Jude, 2 Peter*, 15.

66. Ellis, *Prophecy and Hermeneutic*, 229–230. Cf. Barns, "The Epistle of St. Jude," 393.

67. Bauckham, *Jude, 2 Peter*, 22. Ellis's argument that ἀδελφός (Jude 1) refers to a "co-worker" is critiqued by Bauckham at two points. First, "…it is unlikely that ἀδελφοί in Acts ever means more than 'Christians'"; and second, even if Pauline usage of the term is accepted it "… is not a very secure basis for supporting that ἀδελφὸς Ἰακώβου could be easily understood to mean 'one of James' co-workers'" (25).

68. Martin Luther, "Preface to the Epistles of St. James and St. Jude," in *Luther's Works*, American ed., trans. Charles M. Jacobs, rev. Theodore Bachmann, vol. 35 (Philadelphia: Muhlenberg Press, 1960). Luther's assertion of Jude that "…no one can deny that it is an extract or copy of St. Peter's second epistle…" (397) has not survived the rigors of modern redactional criticism.

69. For a full discussion see Bauckham, *Jude, 2 Peter*, 141–143; Neyrey, *Jude, 2 Peter*, 120–122; Watson, *Invention, Arrangement, and Style*, 160–163. Reicke, *The Epistles of James, Peter, and Jude*, 190, states that "the best assumption is that both epistles derive from a common tradition which may well have been oral rather than written." Robinson's assertion in *Redating*, 192ff. that both books were penned by the same author is interesting, but as Bauckham and Fornburg have adequately demonstrated, the two letters stem from quite distinct circumstances and from distinct hands. See Tord Fornburg, *An Early Church in a Pluralistic Society: A Study of 2 Peter* (Lund: C. W. K. Gleerup, 1976).

70. Wand, *The General Epistles*, 192.

71. Denis Farkasfalvy, "The Ecclesial Setting of Pseudepigraphy in Second Peter and Its Role in the Formation of the Canon," *The Second Century* 5 (1985):3–29. Farkasfalvy argues that the processes of collection, selection, and composition can be seen in 2 Peter. The reference to Paul's letters suggests a collection of at least some of his writings; the exclusion of apostolic prophecy and apocalyptic pseudepigraphy evidences a selection process; and the pseudepigraphal composition of a letter from Simon Peter, a bond-servant and apostle of Jesus Christ" suggests that the author assumes authority and eliminates further encroachments on it.

72. Neyrey, *Jude, 2 Peter*, 121–122. To his credit, Neyrey critiques his own redaction-critical approach to 2 Peter, "The Form and Background of the Polemic in 2 Peter," (Ph.D. diss., Yale University, 1977). Neyrey believes that his study, along with the works of Fornburg, and Bauckham "...have worked from the hypothesis of the priority of Jude... [and] have all added weight to the hypothesis of Jude's priority..., but they have by no means proven it" (122).

73. Watson, *Invention, Arrangement, and Style*, 161–163. Watson argues that Jude could have injected biblical examples into the framework of 2 Peter, been writing to an audience where pseudepigraphal examples carried some argumentative weight, and may have had a more concise writing style.

74. Bauckham, *Jude and the Relatives of Jesus*, 152; See also, Ellis, *Prophecy and Hermeneutic*, 225ff.

75. Watson, *Invention, Arrangement, and Style*, 163. The results of Watson's attempt to wed redactional and rhetorical criticism with a view towards answering the question of the direction of literary dependence are in his own words "mixed... often the priority of neither can be asserted... occasionally the priority of 2 Peter is indicated... however, by a considerable margin, the priority of Jude is strongly affirmed" (189).

76. This consideration also refutes the idea of a common source—if the common source exists, why write Jude?

77. Sidebottom, *James, Jude, 2 Peter*, 74.

78. Chase, "Jude, Epistle of," 804. Chase favors Syrian Antioch as a destination, but as Bauckham argues, that Jude is not accepted into the Syrian canon makes this an unlikely choice. See also J. Chaine, *Les épîtres catholiques: La seconde épître de Saint Pierre, les épîtres des Saint Jean, l épîtres de Saint Jude*, EBib 27 (Paris: Gabalda, 1939): 266–267.

79. See for example Zahn, *Introduction*, 247, who argues that Jude is a circular letter, but then describes characteristics which would better fit a specific situation, e.g., the troublemakers are members of the community, and they make distinctions.

80. Robinson, *Redating*, 170.

81. Fuchs and Reymond, *L'Épître de Saint Jude*, 152–153, provide a succinct review of the possibilities. See also Sidebottom, *Jude*, 73–75.

82. Bauckham, *Jude, 2 Peter*, 16. Bauckham admits that a sure determination of the location and destination of Jude is "largely guesswork."

83. Gunther, "The Alexandrian Epistle," 549.

84. See Rowston, "The Setting of Jude," and Heiligenthal, *Zwischen Henoch und Paulus*.

85. Martin Hengel, *The 'Hellenization' of Judaea in the First Century after Christ* (London: SCM Press, 1989), 54. Cf. Louis H. Feldman, "Hengel's Judaism and Hellenism in Retrospect;" "How Much Hellenism In Jewish Palestine?" *Hebrew Union College Annual* 57 (1986): 83–111. See also, Fergus Miller, "The Background to the Maccabean Revolution; Reflections on Martin Hengel's 'Judaism and Hellenism'," *Journal of Jewish Studies* 22 (1978): 1–21. Feldman critiques Hengel at all of his 22 primary proofs and argues that significant levels of hellenization can only be detected after the time of the Maccabees, and restricted to aristocratic society.

86. Ibid., 55. Hengel states, "Between 30 and 50 CE in Jerusalem there was more creativity and there were more intellectual possibilities 'than are dreamed of in our philosophy'." Hengel's example of the development of christological doctrine taking place within the milieu of Palestinian Judaism is to a large extent confirmed by Bauckham's approach in *Jude and the Relatives of Jesus*.

87. Hengel anticipates this development in the decades soon after the forties: "By contrast, we must assume that there was a degree of regression in the late community under James from the end of the 40s under the pressure of changed political circumstances," (55).

88. Schelkle, *Der Judasbrief*, 138: "The place of the origin of the letter cannot be indicated with safety."

89. Moffatt, 216. Moffatt errs when he states that Jude "... is full of denunciations which sound to a modern more forcible than profitable" (222).

90. So Bauckham and Ellis. Bauckham's argument about this structure in Jude is the driving force behind his whole commentary.

91. Most treatments of Jude 20–23 offer passing comments on the "pastoral concern" of Jude, or on the importance of church discipline, yet this misses the second and perhaps more important thrust of the letter. Desjardins, "The Portrayal of the Dissidents in 2 Peter and Jude," tries to establish that the letter really tells us more about the concerns of the author than about the actual situation; however, his treatment maintains the monolithic thrust of the letter from a different and less verifiable position: the mind of the author.

Notes for Chapter Two

1. Glen H. Stassen, "A Social Theory Model for Religious Social Ethics," *Journal of Religious Ethics*, 5 (Spring 1977): 20. Stassen responds primarily to Ralph Potter, "The Structure of Certain American Christian Responses to the Nuclear Dilemma," (Ph.D. diss., Harvard University, 1965); *War and Moral Discourse* (Richmond: John Knox Press, 1969); "The Logic of Moral Argument," in *Toward a Discipline of Social Ethics*, ed. Paul Deats (Boston: Boston University Press, 1972); and H. D. Aiken, *Reason and Conduct* (New York: Knopf, 1962).

2. Glen H. Stassen, "Critical Variables in Christian Social Ethics," in *Issues in Christian Social Ethics*, ed. Paul D. Simmons (Nashville: Broadman Press, 1980), 57.

3. Ibid.

4. Ibid.

5. Stassen, "Critical Variables," 58. The quadrants represent the four major dimensions involved in ethical argument and decision making. Arrows show the relationship between the primary dimensions.

6. Ibid., 59.

7. Ibid. See also Stassen, "A Social Theory Model," 12. Here, Stassen confronts Aiken, *Reason and Conduct*, 69, who speaks of a "evocative-expressive level" where: "(1) justifying reasons are not stated, and (2) 'no question of justification can possibly arise.'" Stassen critiques Aiken arguing that some particular judgments are capable of reasoned support. Stassen redefines Aiken's definition for a particular judgment: "(1) judgment applies immediately to a particular case or act, and (2) no reasons are given for the judgment"(ibid.).

8. Ibid., 59–60. In "A Social Theory Model," 12, Stassen again engages Aiken, *Reason and Conduct*, who argues that at this level "serious questions are asked and serious answers given in ethical terms...(1) factual appraisals of relevant means and consequences and (2) rules or procedures in relation to which alone the moral relevance of such appraisals can be established" (70).

9. Stassen, "A Social Theory Model," 12.

10. Stassen, "Critical Variables," 60.

11. Ibid., 61. See also, "A Social Theory Model," 12–13. Stassen collapses Potter's four levels of moral reasoning into the two mentioned categories. Potter, "The Structure of Certain American Christian Responses to the Nuclear Dilemma," outlines the following levels: (1) Revelational-authoritative, or divine command, (2) Regular, or rule-deontological, (3) Situational, or act-deontological and act-utilitarian, and (4) Teleological, (368–370).

12. Ibid., 61.

13. Stassen, "A Social Theory Model," 14.

14. Ibid.

15. Stassen, "Critical Variables," 62–63.

16. Stassen, "A Social Theory Model," 14.

17. Ibid.

18. Ibid., 14–15.

19. Stassen, "Critical Variables," 67.

20. Ibid., 68.

21. Ibid.

22. Ibid., 69.

23. Ibid. Stassen cites as an example Henlee Barnette, "Elements of an Ecological Ethic," in *The Church and the Ecological Crisis* (Grand Rapids: Eerdmans, 1972), who characterizes the *nature* of ecological threat as being primarily environmental pollution, the *degree* of the threat as being extensive, and *links* the threat to several causes (e.g., the anthropocentrism of Western culture, the dominance of technology, consumerism, overconsumption, and overpopulation).

24. Ibid. In "A Social Theory Model," 17, Stassen originally postulated a concern with "the individual thinker's view of *governmental* authority...[as being] powerfully determinative" (emphasis added). Here, he expands the definition of authority to include "other potentially authoritative members of the social system."

25. Ibid. Stassen interacts with Stephen Shoemaker, "Christ and the Principalities and Powers in Representative Twentieth Century American Theologians" (Ph.D. diss., The Southern Baptist Theological Seminary, 1978). He cites Shoemaker's outline of four Christian perspectives on principalities and powers: "(1) The tension between the already and the not yet in Christ's victory over the powers...(2) The lordship of Christ as not only subjective but at least partly objective and normative over the authorities... (3) The powers as fallen but not demonized...(4) The powers as potentially demonic when they become idolatrous or unjust" (69–70).

26. Ibid., 70.

27. Stassen, "A Social Theory Model," 18.

28. Ibid., 19.

29. Stassen, "Critical Variables," 71–72. Stassen here confronts H. Edward Everding and Dana W. Wilbanks, *Decision-Making and the Bible* (Valley Forge: Judson Press, 1975), 48–49.

30. Ibid., 72. Stassen articulates the importance of this distinction: "A person holds orthodox *beliefs* about God, but his life indicates that his ultimate *loyalty* is to his money, his automobiles, and his social standing. If only his doctrinal beliefs are analyzed and the faith-loyalties dimension is overlooked, the real disease will be missed."

31. Ibid. Stassen states that "... 96 percent of the distortion in biblical interpretation and ethical decision comes from group loyalties and interests, and only 4 percent comes from minor differences in the wording and translation of the biblical text."

32. Potter, "The Structure of Certain American Christian Responses to the Nuclear Dilemma," 331, cited by Stassen, "A Social Theory Model," 19.

33. For an example of Stassen's model applied to contemporary ethical analysis see Richard D. Axtell, "Ghandian Development Ethics as a Constructive Response to the Modernization of Dependency Debate" (Ph.D. diss., The Southern Baptist Theological Seminary, 1992). Axtell identifies Stassen's classifications as a "cybernetic" model which finds its analytical strength "... by making key variables explicit and analyzing social and cultural outcomes." Axtell emphasizes the "self-correcting" feature of the model which "reveals needed corrections in interpretations of human nature and destiny, love and justice, and social change variables in both realism and liberalism" (45).

Notes for Chapter Three

1. Alexander Roberts and James Donaldson, gen. eds. *The Ante-Nicene Fathers*, 10 vols., rev. A. Cleveland Coxe, American reprint of the Edinburgh Edition (Grand Rapids: Wm. B. Eerdmans, 1985), vol. 10: 424.

2. ANF, vol. 2: *Fathers of the Second Century*.

3. Phillip Schaff, gen. ed. *Nicene and Post-Nicene Fathers*, First Series, 14 vols. (Wm B. Eerdmans, 1983), vol. 2: *St. Augustine's City of God and Christian Doctrine*.

4. NPNF, vol. 6: *St. Augustine Sermon on the Mount, Harmony of the Gospels, and Homilies on the Gospels*, 328.

5. Robert D. Sider, gen. ed., *Collected Works of Erasmus*, 86 vols. (Toronto: University of Toronto Press, 1993), vol. 44: *Paraphrases*, trans. John J. Bateman, 123–130.

6. Ibid., 125.

7. Ibid., 127.

8. Ibid., 124. Bateman argues that "the reference is presumably to Paul in 2 Thess 2:5–12 and 1 Tim 4:1, and to Peter in 2 Pet 2:1 and 3:2–4" (315 n. 1).

9. Ibid., 129.

10. Ibid., 124.

11. Ibid., 129.

12. Martin Luther, "Sermons on the Epistle of St. Jude," in *Luther's Works*, American Edition, trans. Martin H. Bertram, vol. 30: *The Catholic Epistles*, ed. Jaroslav Pelikan (Saint Louis: Concordia Publishing House, 1967), 203.

13. Ibid. See also, "Preface to the Epistle of St. James and St. Jude," in *Luther's Works*, vol. 35:397.

14. Ibid., 210. Luther cites Paul's mention of Jannes and Jambres in 2 Tim. 3:8, as evidence of other NT writers citing non-canonical sources.

15. Luther, "Preface to the Epistles of St. James and St. Jude," 398.

16. Heiligenthal, *Zwischen Henoch und Paulus*, 1.

17. Luther, "Sermons on the Epistle of St. Jude," 203.

18. Ibid., 203–204.

19. Ibid., 205.

20. Luther, "Lectures on Galatians," in *Luther's Works*, vol. 27:48.

21. Luther, "Sermons on the Epistle of St. Jude," 214.

22. John Calvin, *Commentaries on the Catholic Epistles*, trans. and ed. John Owen (Grand Rapids: Wm. B. Eerdmans, 1948).

23. Ibid., 427.

24. Ibid.

25. Ibid., 443.

26. Ibid., 445.

27. Robert M. Grant and David Tracy, *A Short History of the Interpretation of the Bible*, 2nd ed. (Philadelphia: Fortress Press, 1984), 111.

28. Adolf Jülicher, *An Introduction to the New Testament*, trans. J. P. Ward (London: Smith, Elder, & Co., 1904), 14. Jülicher states "F. Schleiermacher's doubts as to the genuineness of 1 Timothy were soon extended to 2 Timothy and Titus; the right of the Epistle to the Hebrews, the Apocalypse, the Catholic Epistles, to bear the names of their supposed authors was denied with ever greater insistence and on ever new grounds."

29. Heiligenthal, *Zwischen Henoch und Paulus*, 3: "Während Baur die Frage nach den unterschiedlichen Positionen in der frühchristlichen Theologie- und Zeitgeschichte noch mit dem einfachen Gegensatz von Juden- und Heidenchristentum, von Paulinismus und Petrinismus beantworten konnte, wurde im Laufe der Zeit die Forschungssituation immer komplexer und unübersichtlicher."

30. Ibid.: "In der Forschungsgeschichte lag im Blick auf den Jude schon immer ein besonderes Interesse auf seiner Beziehung zum Paulinismus. Die 'Tübinger Schule' sah im Jud ein spätes Zeugnis gegen das paulinische Christentum." Heiligenthal points out that E. Renan, *Saint Paul* (Paris: M. Lévy, 1869), 300–303, goes even a step further: "Für ihn was 'Balamm' (Jud 11) eine Anspielung auf Paulus. Von dieser Vermutung leitet er ab, dass der Jud zur Zeit des antiochenischen Zwischenfalls aktuell gegen Paulus geschrieben worden sei"(ibid.).

31. Jülicher, *Introduction*, states that "it is usual to designate the Tübingen writers briefly as 'tendency-critics,' because in the case of every book of the New Testament they inquire first of all into the 'tendency' it was meant to serve" (17).

32. Pfleiderer, *Primitive Christianity*, 251–252.

33. Ibid., 252. Pfleiderer finds confirmation for his thesis in Clement of Alexandria who "...regarded the polemic of the Epistle of Jude as having a prophetic reference." See *Strom*. 3:2:11.

34. Ibid., 254.

35. Ibid. Pfleiderer offers no speculation as to why such an obscure pseudonym is chosen by the author of Jude beyond the suggestion that the name Jude resonated with local tradition or legend.

36. Ibid., 253.

37. Adolf Harnack, *Geschicte Der Altchristlichen Literatur Bis Eusebius*, II/1 (Leipzig: J. C. Hinrichs Verlag, 1958), 466: "Nicht sowohl an die Karpokratianer ist hier zu denken (obgleich Clemens Alex. an sie denkt), als an jene syrisch-palästinensischen Gnostiker ... "

38. Joseph B. Mayor, *The Epistle of St. Jude and the Second Epistle of St. Peter* (London: MacMillan, 1907). Mayor himself writes that he considers the volume on Jude and 2 Peter to be an "appendix" to his commentary on James (vii).

39. Ibid., cxiv. Mayor suggests the relatively early date of A.D. 70–80.

40. Ibid., cli.

41. Ibid., cxiv. Mayor cites Jude's "familiarity" with the "Pauline" language σωτήρ, σωτηρία, κλητοί, and ἅγιοι (cl).

42. Ibid., clii. Mayor's assessment extends to his discussion of Jude's relationship to 2 Peter: "The broad distinction between the two Epistles may be said to be that, while Jude is throughout occupied with the denunciation of evil-doers, except in vv. 1–3 and 20–25, Peter's denunciations are mainly confined to a portion of chapter 2, and the latter dwells more upon the mercy of god as shown even in his punishments" (xvi).

43. Jülicher, *Introduction*, 231. He suggests a date between A.D. 100 and 180, but not "too late" because "...the author's mood seems to be one of astonishment and indignation at this ungodliness" (ibid.)

44. Ibid., 203. Yet in his more specific discussion of Jude, Jülicher recognizes the more situation specific origin of Jude and postulates: "Yet in itself there is nothing impossible in the theory that it was addressed to a single church or group of churches, which, on receiving the document, found themselves fully enough described in verse 1" (229).

45. Charles Bigg, *The Epistles of St. Peter and St. Jude*, The International Critical Commentary, 41 (Edinburgh: T & T Clark, 1901).

46. Ibid., 311.

47. Ibid., 312.

48. Ibid., 313. Contra Jülicher who takes the opponents to be "...as Carpocratians, or a Archontics, or as 'a school of Gnostics which afterwards disappeared." Bigg argues that "every word of this [Jülicher's] reasoning is disputable in the highest degree," but that the opponents "...may be called Gnostics, at the cost of a slight anachronism" (ibid.)

49. Ibid., 321–322.

50. F. H. Chase, "Jude, Epistle of," *Dictionary of the Bible*, vol. 2, ed. James Hastings (New York: Charles Scribner's Sons, 1902). Chase maintains the priority of Jude, and argues for Jude's perception of the situation linked to the situation faced by Paul in Corinth.

51. Theodor Zahn, *Introduction to the New Testament*, trans. Melancton W. Jacobus (New York: Charles Scribner's Sons, 1917). Zahn maintains the priority of 2 Peter, and argues that 2 Peter and Jude are written to the same group of churches.

52. James Moffatt, *The General Epistles of James, Peter, and Judas* (New York: Harper and Brothers Publishers, 1928).

53. J. W. C. Wand, *The General Epistles of St. Peter and St. Jude* (London: Methuen & Co., 1934).

54. See for example Beasley-Murray, *The General Epistles*; J. C. Beker, "Jude" in *The Interpreter's Dictionary of the Bible*, ed. G. A. Buttrick, vol. 2 (New York: Abingdon Press, 1962): 1009–1011; G. H. Boobyer, "Jude," in *Peake's Commentary on the Bible*, ed. M. Black and H. H. Rowley (London: Nelson, 1963); Jean Cantinat, *The Catholic Epistles*, in *Introduction to the New Testament*, ed. A. Robert and A. Feuillet (New York: Desclee, 1965); Cranfield, *I & II Peter and Jude*; Kelly, *A Commentary on the Epistles of Peter and Jude*; Leaney, *The Letters of Peter and Jude*; Reicke, *The Epistles of James, Peter and Jude*; Sidebottom, *James, Jude and 2 Peter*; and Ray Summers, "Jude," in *The Broadman Bible Commentary*, ed. Clifton J. Allen, vol. 12 (Nashville: Broadman Press, 1972): 232–239.

55. See chapter 1 note 4 above.

56. E. Earle Ellis, "Prophecy and Hermenuetic in Jude," in *Prophecy and Hermeneutic in Early Christianity*, WUNT 18 (Tübingen: J.C.B. Mohr [Paul Siebeck], 1978), 221–236.

57. Ibid., 221. Ellis argues that these "expositions employ not only quotations but also explicit and implicit midrashim on the Old Testament as their authoritative texts" (ibid.).

58. Ibid., 225. Ellis cites catchwords which "join quotation to quotation (e.g., κρίσις 6,9,15), quotation to commentary (e.g., λαλεῖν, 15,16), quotation to Jude's introduction (e.g., κύριος, 4,15), quotation to Jude's final application (e.g., σώζω, 5,23), or they may join all four elements (τηρεῖν, 1,6,13,21; κύριος, 4,5,14,17,21)" (ibid.).

59. Ibid. This approach has been received most favorably by Bauckham, *Jude, 2 Peter*. See below.

60. Ibid., 226. Ellis finds similar expressions of this type of midrashic structure and theme in the NT and in the biblical exposition found at Qumran.

61. Ibid., 230. Ellis argues that the Jude of Acts 15 fits certain characteristics which are demonstrated in the commentary style which he identifies in the text of the Epistle. Cf. 32–33 above.

62. Ibid., 236.

63. Duane F. Watson, *Invention, Arrangement, and Style: Rhetorical Criticism of Jude and 2 Peter*, SBLDS 104 (Atlanta: Scholars Press, 1988). Cf. Stephan J. Joubert, "Persuasion in the Letter of Jude," *Journal for the Study of the New Testament* 58 (1995): 75–87.

64. Ibid., 79.

65. Ibid., 32.

66. Ibid., vii.

67. Ibid., 33.

68. Ibid., 71.

69. Ibid., 31, emphasis added.

70. Thomas R. Wolthuis, "Jude and the Rhetorician: A Dialogue on the Rhetorical Nature of the Epistle of Jude," *Calvin Theological Journal* 24 (1989): 126–134. Watson, *Invention, Arrangement, and Style*, points out that the origin of Jude's rhetorical skill, "whether gained from daily interaction with verbal and written culture and/or from formal training is impossible to determine" (79).

71. J. Daryl Charles, *Literary Strategy in the Epistle of Jude* (Scranton: University of Scranton Press, 1993). See also, Charles, "'Those' and 'these': The Use of the OT in the Epistle of Jude," *Journal for the Study of the New Testament* 38 (1990): 109–124; and "The Use of Traditional Material in the Epistle of Jude," *Bulletin of Biblical Research* 4 (1994): 1–14.

72. Ibid., 167.

73. Ibid.

74. Ibid.

75. Ibid., 170. See Henning Paulsen, *Der Zweite Petrusbrief und der Judasbrief*, Kritisch-exegetischer Kommentar über das Neue Testament, ed. H. A. W. Meyer (Göttingen: Vandenhoeck & Ruprecht, 1992). Paulsen resonates with Charles' emphasis on the relationship between form and content: "Darin ist die Theologie des Textes anwesend: Es geht dem Vf. in solcher Konfiguration um die grundsätzliche Bearbeitung einer kritischen Situation seiner EmpfängerInnen" (41). "Insofern is den Überlegungen bei Charles zustimmen, die von einer 'indivisibility of form and content' ausgehen" (41 n. 5).

76. Ibid.

77. Ibid., 167.

78. Douglas J. Rowston, "The Setting of the Letter of Jude" (Th.D. diss., The Southern Baptist Theological Seminary, 1971). This helpful characterization of the struggle faced by Jude is picked up in chapters four and five. The tension between eschatology and ecclesiology speaks directly to the basic question behind this analysis; namely, how does God's action in history determine ethical behavior within the believing community?

79. Ibid., 5.

80. Ibid.

81. Ibid., 155.

82. Ibid., 119.

83. Cf. Bauckham, *Jude, 2 Peter*, 11: "Jude's apocalyptic is not at all self-conscious. It is the worldview within which he naturally thinks and which he takes for granted his readers accept."

84. Walter Grundmann, *Der Brief des Judas und der zweite Brief des Petrus*, THKNT 15 (Berlin: Evangelische Verlagsanstallt, 1974).

85. Ibid., 2: "...die Verfasser des Judas- und des 2 Petrusbriefes, kaum auf ihre Lehre einlassen, sondern ihren Missbrauch der Freiheit in ausschweifendem Leben und überheblichem Verhalten den Menschen und Mächten gegenüber bekämpfen."

86. Ibid., 5–6: "Aus der Polemik der beiden Briefe geht hervor, dass sie ihre Freiheit ausleben in Verachtung kosmischer Mächte, gemeindlicher Ordnung und ethisch bindender Gebote."

87. Ibid., 8: "So bedeutsam der harte Zugriff des Urteils ist, so klar er sichtbar macht, dass die Christenheit ohne den ethischen Lebensernst, wie er durch Gottes Gebot gegoten ist... Sie ist um so ernster, als der Verfasser des Judasbriefes auf jede Auseinandersetzung mit ihrer Lehre verzichtet und sich auf den ethischen Vorwurf beschränkt."

88. Ibid., 6: "Sie äussern das in einer Lehre, die sie in den Gemeinden verbreiten, in die sie gekommen sind. Sie scheint aus hellenistisch-jüdischen Weisheitsüberlieferungen herzurühren..."

89. Ibid., 19.

90. Ibid., 6: "Judas kann sich keinen Gottesglauben denken, der das Leben nicht unter das bindende Gebot Gottes stellt. Es gibt keine Freiheit, die nur Freiheit von etwas wäre; vielmehr ist die Freiheit des Evangeliums zugleich Freiheit zu etwas..." Grundmann points to this kind of freedom expressed in Paul (Gal 3:13f; 4:4–6; Rom 8:2–4; 6:12–23; 7:1–6; 1 Cor 6:12; 10:23; 9:14–23).

91. Henning Paulsen, *Der Zweite Petrusbrief und der Judasbrief*, Kritisch-exegetischer Kommentar über das Neue Testament, XII/2 (Göttingen: Vandenhoeck & Ruprecht, 1992); Anton Vögtle, *Der Judasbrief/Der Zweite Petrusbrief*, Evangelisch-Katholischer Kommentar zum Neuen Testament, 22 (Düsseldorf: Benzinger Verlag; Neukirchen-Vluyn: Neukircher Verlag, 1994).

92. Paulsen, *Der Judasbrief*, 51: "Die Theologie des Jud wird nur dann richtig verstenden, wenn sie die Zuordnung von gegebenem Fundament der pistis und Polemik gegen die Haretiker als durch den Verfasser gewollt und so in der Spache bedingt beingt begreift." On Bauckham, see below.

93. Vögtle's primary foil is Richard Bauckham, whose antinomian characterization of the problem faced by Jude is juxtaposed to Vögtle's emphasis on the conflict between orthodoxy and heresy. See chapter 1 note 42.

94. Vögtle, *Der Judasbrief*, 95–96: "Das enthusiastische Bewusstsein ihres Geistbesitzes, das auch eine gewisse Erhabenheit über moralische Zwänge erklärt..." Vögtle links these characteristics to the realized eschatology which is expressed in other writings near the end of the 1st century.

95. Ibid., 95: "...die für unsere Kenntnis ausgeprägteste Modell der Ketzer polemik in der frühen Kirche hervorbrachte."

96. Stassen, "Critical Variables," 72. See chapter 2 note 33.

97. Jerome Neyrey, *Jude, 2 Peter*, The Anchor Bible, vol. 37c (New York: Doubleday, 1993).

98. Ibid., 3. Neryey states: "We do not consider these perspectives intrusive into the interpretive process, but rather friendly and compatible templates which help us to see what would otherwise escape notice."

99. Ibid., 3–20. Neyrey provides a brief introductory discussion and bibliography for each of the models employed.

100. Ibid., 52.

101. Ibid., 32–42.

102. See chapter 2 note 32.

103. Ibid., 7. Neyrey cites among others: David Daube, "Disgrace," *The New Testament and Rabbinic Judaism* (New York: Arno Press, 1973), 301–324; Bruce J. Malina and Jerome Neyrey, "Honor and Shame in Luke-Acts: Pivotal Values of the Mediterranean World," in *The World of Luke-Acts. Models for Interpretation* (Peabody, MA: Hendrickson, 1991), 25–65; and J. G. Peristiani, ed., *Honor and Shame: The Values of Mediterranean Society* (Chicago: University of Chicago Press, 1966).

104. Richard Bauckham, *Jude, 2 Peter*, Word Biblical Commentary, vol. 50 (Waco: Word Books, 1983); *Jude and the Relatives of Jesus in the Early Church* (Edinburgh: T & T Clark, 1990).

105. See above, 5–8.

106. Bauckham, *Jude and the Relatives of Jesus*, 160–161. See above, 7.

107. Ibid., 162. Emphasis added. Cf. Grundmann, *Der Brief des Judas*, 15–19. Bauckham cites Grundmann's "...observation that, in abandoning reasoned discussion and concentrating on attacking his opponent's moral character, Jude is a typical Jewish Christian" (156).

108. Ibid., 154.

109. Ibid., 157.

110. Bauckham, *Jude, 2 Peter*, 32. Bauckham dismisses the objective use of πίστις and argues that "Jude's readers are to contend, not for some particular formulation of Christian belief, but for the central Christian message of salvation through Jesus Christ" (33).

111. Bauckham, *Jude and the Relatives of Jesus*, 157.

112. Ibid., 165.

113. Ibid., 159. Cf. Vögtle, *Der Judasbrief*, 7.

114. Bauckham, *Jude, 2 Peter*, 5, relies heavily on Ellis, "Prophecy and Hermeneutic in Jude," and J. Carmignac, "Le document de Qumran sur Melkisédeq," *Revue de Qumran* 7 (1969–71): 360–361, in his discussion of the resemblance of Jude's exegetical method to the thematic pesherim found at Qumran. Bauckham cautiously accepts the initial similarities between Jude and some of the Qumran documents, but offers the following distinctives: Qumran persherim (1) do not deal with apocryphal books, or oral prophecy; (2) do not use scripture summaries rather than actual citations; (3) do not employ typology.

115. Bauckham, *Jude and the Relatives of Jesus*, 158. See also, *Jude, 2 Peter*, 114–117.

116. In particular see Bauckham's chapter on "Jude's Christology," in *Jude and the Relatives of Jesus*, 281–314.

117. Bauckham, *Jude, 2 Peter*, 8.

118. Roman Heiligenthal, *Zwischen Henoch und Paulus: Studien zum theologiegeschichtlichen Ort des Judasbriefes*, TANZ 6 (Tübingen: Franke, 1992). See also, Heiligenthal, "Der Judasbrief: Aspekte der Forschung in den letzten Jahrzehnten," *Theologische Rundschau* 51 (1986): 117–129, and "Die Weisheitsschrift der Kairoer Geniza und der Judasbrief," *Zeitschrift für Religions- und Geistesgeschichte* 44 (1992): 356–361.

119. Heiligenthal, "Der Judasbrief," 129: "Wenn wir auf die letzten Jahre der Forschung am Jud zurückblicken, so lässt sich allgemein ein verstärktes Interesse und eine veränderte Sicht-weise feststellen. Als Zeugnis der Theologiegeschichte wird er wieder mehr ernst genommen. Auch versucht man sich an einer stärker pragmatischen Interpretation, die seiner Entstehungs situation eher gerecht wird. Wer wünschen dem Jud, dass er noch mehr aus dem Schattendasein heraustritt und die Zeit seiner pauschalen Verurteilung endgültig vorüber ist."

120. Heiligenthal, *Zwischen Henoch und Paulus*, 12–13: "Die Position des Jud im Blick auf die Engelverehrung kann wichtige Hinweise auf den Ort des Briefes innerhalb der früchristlichen Theologiegeschichte geben. . . . Die Untersuchung der christologischen und ekkleiologischen Begrifflichkeit innerhalb des Jud kann wichtige Hinweise auf Übereinstimmungen und Besonderheiten innerhalb der theologischen Landschaft des frühen Christentums geben."

121. Ibid., 13: "Die theologische Entwicklung nach Paulus lässt sich grundsätzlich in assimilatioins- freundiliche (Hellenisierung) und assimilationsfeindliche Tendenzen (Judenchristentum) unterteilen."

122. Ibid., 156: "Er vertritt ein Judenchristentum, das in Jesus den kommenden Kyrios sieht, der mit seinen Engeln und der Gemeinde eine Gemeinschaft der 'Heiligen' bildet, die sich von aller Unreinheit freihalten soll. Engel lehre und Reinheits affasung sind Ausdruck einer pharisäischen Frömmigkeit."

123. Ibid., 157: "Der Jud ist eine judenchristliche Schrift. Seine Trägerkreise sind unter christlichen Pharisäern zu suchen, die Teile der Henoch über lieferung als einen wesentlichen Bestandteil ihrer Tradition ansahen. Si bildeten Gemeinden, die sich als 'familia dei' wahrscheinlich in form eines 'Lehrhauses' organisierten und diese gegen Assimilierungstendenzen ander geprägter Christen zu verteidigen suchten."

124. Ibid. "Die christlichen Elemente der Theologie des Jud sind theologiegeschichtlich alt und könnten aus dem Umfeld einer antiochenischen Normaltheologie stammen."

125. See Heiligenthal, "Die Weisheitsschrift der Kairoer Geniza und der Judasbrief." Here, Heiligenthal convincingly articulates the "social dimension of faith for Jude's community" (357).

126. Ibid., 358: "...nach der es der 'Glaube' ist, der die Brüder zu einem 'Haus' zusammenschliesst. Hierbei eröffnet der Glaube die Möglichkeit sozialer Identität, nach aussen ist er das zentrale Unterscheidungskriterium, das Abgrenzungen von der Umwelt ermöglicht. Auch in der Weisheitsschrift hat 'Glaube' diese zentrale Funktion der Zugehörigkeit, also beinahe ekklesiologischen Charakter." Heiligenthal cites *Wisdom Writing from Cairo Geniza* 4:7ff.: ". . . and do not harm any brother who believes in the God of Israel, (8) even when there is no knowledge in him. Even then a little faith is justification."

127. See N. T. Wright, *The Climax of the Covenant: Christ and the Law in Pauline Theology* (Edinburgh: T & T Clark, 1991), 2–3. Wright argues that Paul likewise conceives of faith as the "boundary-marker" which sets covenant community apart from both pagans and Jews.

128. Heiligenthal, *Zwischen Henoch und Paulus*, 157.

129. Ibid., 166: "Es geht ihm um die Bewahrung der Gemeinde als 'familia dei,' um ihren Schutz vor assimilier- enden Einflüssen." For example, Heiligenthal argues that apocalyptic eschatology is applied to pneumatological claims of direct entrance to salvation.

130. Heiligenthal's suggestion that the situation faced by the author of Jude is directly linked to the outgrowth of misunderstood Pauline theology at Colossae is speculative at best. Heiligenthal himself offers this caveat: "...eine genaue Bestimmung seines Entsehungsortes erscheint mir aber auch weiterhin als äusserst spekulativ" (ibid., 11–12); yet he proceeds to posit

the Colossae connection. The effort to link the problem faced by Jude with Pauline theology reveals Heiligenthal's bias in making Paul normative for the early Christian community. Cf. Bauckham, *Jude, 2 Peter*, 8, who argues that this "...depends on the too ready assumption that ideas and terminology which Paul uses are distinctively Pauline, so that other writers who use them must be dependent on Paul or 'Paulinism.'"

131. Luther and Calvin are included here as examples of individuals who allowed their own loyalties, interests, and trusts to determine their interpretation of the text. To some extent, each of the scholars examined is guilty of this phenomenon. I am fully aware that, more often than not, this tendency clouds my own approach to the Epistle of Jude.

Notes for Chapter Four

1. See 24-26 above.

2. On ecclesiology as a theological category, see Hendrikus Berkhof, *Christian Faith: An Introduction to the Study of the Faith*, trans. Sierd Woudstra (Grand Rapids: Wm. B. Eerdmans, 1986), 343–415; Stanley Grenz, *Theology for the Community of God* (Nashville: Broadman & Holmann, 1994), 601–705.

3. Christopher Rowland, *The Open Heaven: A Study of Apocalyptic in Judaism and Early Christianity* (London: SPCK, 1982).

4. Joachim Gnilka, "Apocalyptik und Ethik: Die Kategorie der Zukunft als Anweisung für sittliches Handeln," in *Neues Testament und Ethik: Festschrift Für Rudolf Schnackenburg*, ed. Helmut Merklin (Freiburg/Basel/Wien: Herder, 1989), 464–481. "Das Reich Gottes ist nicht bloss zukunftig- eschatologisch- jenseitig- wenn es dies auch primar ist-, sondern es will auch schon in dieser Welt mit seinen heilenden un rettenden Draften wirksam werden. . . . So bleibt die höffende Orientierung der christlichen Existenz auf diese absolute Zukunft hin, die Impetus sittlichen Handelns ist" (480–481).

5. Cf. Rowston, "The Setting of the Letter of Jude"; Bauckham, *Jude, 2 Peter*; Heiligenthal, *Zwischen Henoch und Paulus*.

6. W. S. Vorster, "1 Enoch and the Jewish Literary Setting of the New Testament: A Study in Text types," *Studies in 1 Enoch and the New Testament: Proceedings of the 19th Meeting of the New Testament Society of South Africa, Neotestamentica* 17 (1983), 1.

7. See P. D. Hanson, "Apocalypse, Genre," and "Apocalypticism," *International Dictionary of the Bible*, Supp. (Nashville: Abingdon, 1976), 27–34. Also, M. E. Stone, "Lists of Revealed Things in the Apocalyptic Literature," in *Magnalia Dei: The Mighty Acts of God*, ed. F. M. Cross, W. E. Lemke, P. D. Miller, Jr. (Garden City: Doubleday, 1976), 414–452.

8. See for example, John J. Collins, ed., "Apocalypse: The Morphology of a Genre," *Semeia* 14 (1979): 9. The definition of an Apocalypse established by John J. Collins and the Apocalypse Group of the Society of Biblical Literature's Genres Project is as follows: "Apocalypse is a genre of revelatory literature with a narrative framework, in which a revelation is mediated by an otherworldly being to a human recipient, disclosing a transcendent reality which is both temporal, insofar as it envisages eschatological salvation, and spatial, insofar as it involves another spiritual world."

9. John J. Collins, "Introduction: Towards the Morphology of a Genre," *Semeia* 14 (1979): 4. Emphasis added. See also, David Hellholm, ed., *Apocalypticism in the Mediterranean World and the Near East* (Tübingen: J. C. B. Mohr [Paul Siebeck], 1983).

10. Collins, "Introduction," 4.

11. William A. Beardslee, "New Testament Apocalyptic in Recent Interpretation," *Interpretation* 25 (1971): 422. Beardslee states: "The Qumran scrolls make it crystal clear that... [the examination of apocalyptic in a wide variety of forms] has to be the procedure. The literary form of the apocalypse was very well-known at Qumran... .But motifs found in those books so thoroughly permeate other literary forms, such as Hymns, the Manual of Discipline, and the War Scroll, that there can be no question of limiting apocalyptic to what can be derived only from the literary form of the apocalypse."

12. Mitchell G. Reddish, ed., *Apocalyptic Literature: A Reader* (Nashville: Abingdon Press, 1990), 19.

13. Ibid., 23.

14. Beardslee, "New Testament Apocalyptic," points to several important factors in the apocalyptic perception of reality: (1) the minority status of the community in question; (2) meaning or existence of the community is linked to the end time; (3) an emphasis on the end being at hand; (4) a realization that humanity exists in time; and (5) a belief in esoteric revelations (422ff.).

15. W. S. Vorster, "1 Enoch and the Jewish Literary Setting of the New Testament," 1–14.

16. It is referred to by Clement of Alexandria, *Fragm. in. Ep. Jd.* on verse 9; and Origen, *De Princ.* 3:2:1.

17. On the critical issues surrounding the *Assumption of Moses*, see R. H. Charles, *The Apocrypha and Pseudepigrapha of the Old Testament in English*, vol. 2 (Oxford: Clarendon Press, 1913); J. Priest, "Testament of Moses," in *The Old Testament Pseudepigrapha*, ed. James H. Charlesworth, vol. 1 (Garden City: Doubleday, 1983):919–926; Richard Bauckham, *Jude, 2 Peter*, with particular emphasis on his excursus dealing with the background of Jude 9 (65–76); George W. Nicklesburg, ed., *Studies on the Testament of Moses*, SBLSCS 4

(Cambridge: Society of Biblical Literature, 1973); and David Russell, *Old Testament Pseudepigrapha: Prophets and Patriarchs in Early Judaism* (London: SCM Press, 1987).

18. Johannes Tromp, *The Assumption of Moses: A Critical Edition with Commentary* (New York: E. J. Brill, 1993). Prior to Tromp, see E. -M. Laperrousaz, *Le Testament de Moïse*, *Semitica* 19 (1970):1–40.

19. Tromp, *Assumption of Moses*, 115.

20. Ibid., 116. Tromp cites D. M. Rhodes, "The Assumption of Moses and Jewish History: 4 B.C.– A.D. 48," in *Studies in the Testament of Moses*, ed. G. W. Nickelsburg SBLSCS 4 (Cambridge: Society of Biblical Literature, 1973):58. In this same volume, see also, John J. Collins, "The Date and Provenance of the Testament of Moses," (15–32); George W. E. Nickelsburg, "An Antiochan Date for the Testament of Moses" (33–37).

21. Tromp, *Assumption of Moses*, 117.

22. Ibid.

23. Cf. Anitra Bingham Kolenkow, "The Assumption of Moses as a Testament," in *Studies in the Testament of Moses*, ed. G. W. E. Nickelsburg, SBLSCS 4 (Cambridge: Society of Biblical Literature, 1973): 71–77.

24. Bauckham, *Jude, 2 Peter*, 65–76; *Jude and the Relatives of Jesus* (235–280); Cf. S. E. Loewenstamm, "The Death of Moses," in *Studies in the Testament of Abraham*, ed. G. W. E. Nickelsburg, SBLSCS 4 (Missoula, MT: Scholars Press, 1976): 185–217.

25. Tromp, *The Assumption of Moses*, 270.

26. Ibid. All citations from Charlesworth, *Old Testament Pseudepigrapha*, vol. 1.

27. Tromp, *Assumption of Moses*, 276. Tromp points to 4QAmram 1:10–11 which demonstrates the motif of struggle between good and bad angels was known in the first century: "[I saw] in a vision, a vision in a dream, that two of them were speaking about me, . . . and they had a great fight over me." See J. T. Milik, "4Q Visions de 'Amram et une citation d'Origène," *Revue Biblique* 79 (1972): 79.

28. Ibid., 119. Tromp cites *As. Mos.* 7:3–10 and suggests that it must be "... acknowledged that [the author] has spoken in this passage with disdain about the 'gentlemen in power' in general terms, irrespective of any religious or political distinctions among rulers."

29. Contrary to most comments on κρίσιν . . . βλασφημίας Bauckham, *Jude, 2 Peter*, 60, does not see a genitive of quality or adjectival genitive; rather he suggests the following translation: "to condemn for slander." Cf. C. F. D. Moule, *An Idiom Book of New Testament Greek*

(Cambridge: Cambridge University Press, 1959), 175. Moule suggests an adjectival genitive which may reflect a Semitic idiom—a "vituperative verdict."

30. Margaret Barker, *The Lost Prophet: The Book of Enoch and Its Influence on Christianity* (London: SPCK, 1988). Barker states that ". . . the Book of Enoch has long been recognized as the most important Jewish writing from the New Testament period" (1). For treatment of critical issues, see E. Isaac, "1 (Ethiopic Apocalypse of) Enoch," in *Pseudepigrapha of the Old Testament*, 5–12; Michael Knibb, *Ethiopic Book of Enoch: A New Edition in the Light of the Aramaic Dead Sea Fragments*, 2 vols. (Oxford: Clarendon Press, 1978); Michael Knibb, "The Ethiopic Book of Enoch," in *Outside the Old Testament*, ed. M. De Jonge (Cambridge: Cambridge University Press, 1985), 26–55.

31. Sidebottom, *James, Jude, and 2 Peter*, 90. Sidebottom notes that ". . . the quotation from 1 Enoch was proof to many in Jerome's time that the epistle of Jude was not inspired scripture."

32. Ellis, "Prophecy and Hermeneutic in Jude," 224, argues that the references to *As. Mos.* and *Enoch* in verses 9 and 14ff ". . . are apocryphal elaborations of the Old Testament... which [are] regarded as inspired in [their] own right and/or as faithful interpretation of inspired teaching." Cf. Walter M. Durnett, "The Hermeneutics of Jude and 2 Peter: The Use of Ancient Jewish Traditions," *Journal of the Evangelical Theological Society* 31 (1988): 289. Durnett suggests that ". . . in the early Church there existed the problem of the propriety or impropriety of citing this sort of literature in public documents... very likely Jude and 2 Peter, respectively, reflect different views regarding this issue."

33. J. T. Milik, *The Books of Enoch* (Oxford: Clarendon Press, 1976). In particular, the absence of the *Similitudes* (37–71) from the Aramaic fragments leaves open the debate about the importance of a heavenly Son of Man figure for the first century Palestinian milieu. Cf. Margaret Barker, *The Lost Prophet*, 13, who contends that it is dangerous to take the absence of a particular text from Qumran as absolute proof that such a text did not exist prior to the turn of the era. To suggest that the *Similitudes* are a late composition because they are not at Qumran requires us to assume that the Qumran library had a copy of all the Enochic writings, and that the library remained untouched until the second century. In Barker's own words, ". . . it would be very dangerous to assume that what was not there in the 1950's had never been there in the first place"(ibid.).

34. See George R. Beasley-Murray, *Jesus and the Kingdom of God* (Grand Rapids: Wm. B. Eerdmans, 1986), 52ff. Beasley-Murray rejects the notion that 37–71 reflect Christian interpolation because there is no specifically Christian doctrine expressed. Noting the Daniel 7 background of the Son of Man imagery, Beasley-Murray holds that no Christian writer would identify Enoch as the Son of Man. Beasley-Murray points to the historical references in 56:5–7 and 67:7–13 and suggests a time of composition soon after the death of Herod in the first half of the first century. Beasley-Murray's treatment keeps open the possibility of parallel lines of development in the first century which stem from a particular understanding of Daniel 7 and the function of "the one like a Son of Man."

35. Compare treatments prior and subsequent to the discovery of fragments at Qumran: Charles, *The Book of Enoch* (Oxford: Clarendon Press, 1983), late-early pre-Maccabean; Reddish, *Apocalyptic Literature*, 146, early second or late third century.

36. See Barker, *The Older Testament*, and *The Lost Prophet*. Barker's attempt to push back the genesis of the religious themes in *Enoch* to the foundational strata of theological reflection in pre-Deuteronomistic Israel is intriguing. While it is possible to take issue with Barker's creative exegesis, her imaginative lines of connection, and her provocative conclusions, it is difficult to argue against her primary assertion that the Enochic tradition stands at a more foundational level of influence than previously allowed by scholarship.

37. Reddish, *Apocalyptic Literature*, 144.

38. Tord Fornburg, *An Early Church in a Pluralistic Society*, 51.

39. Barker, *The Lost Prophet*, 1.

40. Reddish, *Apocalyptic Literature*, 144.

41. Durnett, "The Hermeneutics of Jude," 289.

42. Charles, "'Those' and 'These': The Use of the OT in the Epistle of Jude," 190.

43. Ibid.

44. Bauckham, *Jude, 2 Peter*, 7. Bauckham cites, for example: (1) verse 12 to Prov 25:14; (2) verse 13 to Isa 57:30, but the LXX does not give the meaning Jude adopts; (3) verse 11 to Num 26:9; (4) verse 12 to Ezek 34:2; (5) verse 23 to Amos 4:11 and Zech 3:3 where the vocabulary fails to correspond to the LXX. Bauckham asserts that "the evidence show conclusively that it was the Hebrew Bible with which Jude was really familiar."

45. Rowston, "The Setting of the Letter of Jude," 44. Rowston outlines the following signs of indebtedness to the OT in Jude: (1) verse 5 to Exod 12:51; Num 14:29f, 35 (2) verse 6 to Gen 6:1–4; (3) verse 7 to Gen 19:4–25; (4) verse 9 to Zech 3:2; (5) verse 11 to Gen 4:3–8, Num 31:16; 16:19–35; (6) verse 12 to Ezek 34:8; Prov 25:14; (7) verse 13 to Isa 57:20 (Hebrew Text); (8) verse 16 to Lev 19:15 (LXX); and (9) verse 23 to Amos 4:11; Zech 3:2.

46. Ellis, "Prophecy and Hermeneutic in Jude." See above, 44–45.

47. Bauckham, *Jude, 2 Peter*, 46. Bauckham points to other examples where this schema is employed: Sir 16:7–10; CD 2:17–3:12; 3 Macc 2:4–7; *T. Napt.* 3:4–5; *m. Sanh.* 10:3; 2 Pet 2:4–8.

48. Ibid.

49. Ibid., 49.

50. Sidebottom, *James, Jude, 2 Peter*, 85.

51. See Bruce Metzger, *A Textual Commentary on the New Testament* (New York: United Bible Society, 1971), 832. The variant readings Ἰησοῦς and ὁ Ἰησοῦς are "difficult to the point of impossibility." The interesting reading of P⁷², θεὸς Χριστός may be a scribal blunder of the intended θεοῦ χριστός, "God's anointed one" (ibid.). Bauckham, *Jude, 2 Peter*, argues "it is not likely that Jude used Ἰησοῦς of the preexistent Christ," (43); but rather, ". . . because in his typological application of these OT events to the present it is the Lord Jesus who has saved his people the church and will be the judge of apostates" (49). Cf. Jarl Fossum, "Kyrios Jesus as the Angel of the Lord in Jude 5–7," *New Testament Studies* 33 (1987): 226–243, who argues that ". . . Jude some fifty years before Justin Martyr was the first to use 'Jesus' as a name of the Son also in his pre-existence."

52. Fornburg, *An Early Church in a Pluralistic Society*, 51.

53. Cf. T. Francis Glasson, *Greek Influence in Jewish Eschatology* (London: SPCK, 1961), 62ff. Glasson draws lines of connection between the Watchers story in *1 Enoch* and the Titans of Greek mythology: "Though there are basic differences between the Titans and the fallen angels of Enoch and other Jewish writings, it may well be that the Jews drew upon the Titan lore of the Greeks in depicting the doom of the angels."

54. Ibid. With regard to identifying the sinners as angels Fornburg cites Gen 6:2 LXX Codex A; *1 Enoch* 6:2; *Jub.* 5:1–10; *2 Apoc. Bar.* 56:10–15; Josephus, *Ant.* 1:73. With regard to the nature of their sin, *1 Enoch* 12:4. With regard to their punishment, *1 Enoch* 10:4–5; 13:1.

55. Sidebottom, *James, Jude, 2 Peter*, 86. Bauckham, *Jude, 2 Peter*, calls Sodom and Gomorrah "... the paradigm case of divine judgment (Deut 29:23; Isa 1:9; 13:19; Jer 23:14; 49:18; 50:40; Lam 4:6; Hos 11:8; Amos 4:11; Zeph 2:9; Sir 16:8; 3 Macc 2:5; *Jub.* 16:6,9; 20:5; 22:22; 36:10; *T. Asher* 7:1 Philo, *Quaest. in Gen.* 4:51; Josephus, *BJ* 5.566; Matt 10:15; 11:24; Mark 6:11; Luke 10:12; 17:29)" (53).

56. Bauckham, *Jude, 2 Peter*, 54. Bauckham cites the condemnation of the Sodomites "hatred of strangers (Wis 19:14–15; Josephus, *Ant.* 1:194; *Pirqe R. El.* 25), their pride and selfish affluence (Ezek 16:49–50; 3 Macc 2:5; Josephus, *Ant.* 1:194; Philo, *Abr.* 134; *Tg. Ps.-J.* Gen 13:13; 18:20), or their sexual immorality in general (*Jub.* 16:5–6; 20:5; *T. Levi* 14:6; *T. Benj.* 9:1)."

57. Charles, "'Those' and 'These': The Use of the OT in the Epistle of Jude," 117.

58. Rowston, "The Setting of the Letter of Jude," 47.

59. Sidebottom, *James, Jude, 2 Peter*, 89

60. Kelly, *A Commentary On the Epistles of Peter and Jude*, 266. Kelly also cites *Tg. Yer. I*, Gen 4:7 where Cain "...is the first cynic to say, 'There is no judgment, no judge, no future life; no reward will be given to the righteous, and no judgment on the wicked.'"

61. Ibid.

62. Charles, "'Those' and 'These': The Use of the OT in the Epistle of Jude," 116.

63. Rowston, "The Setting of the Letter of Jude," 39.

64. Sidebottom, *James, Jude, 2 Peter*, 89.

65. Kelly, *A Commentary on the Epistles of Peter and Jude*, 267–268. Kelly traces the development of the tradition through Deut 23:4; Neh 13:2; Rev 2:14; Philo *Vit. Mos.* 1:268; *Migr. Abr.* 113ff; Josephus *Ant.* 4:118.

66. Ibid., 268.

67. Bauckham, *Jude, 2 Peter*, 83.

68. Ibid. Bauckham cites: Pseudo-Philo *Bib. Ant.* 16:1; *Tg. Pseudo-Jonathan* Num 16:1–2.

69. Bauckham, *Jude, 2 Peter*, 80. Bauckham cites the use of the expression in the LXX: 3 Kgdms 15:26; 15:34; 16:2; 19; 26; 4 Kgdms 8:18; 27; 16:3; 2 Chron 11:17; 21:6; Ezek 23:31; where "...it means to follow someone's moral example." Cf. G. H. Boobyer, "The Verbs in Jude 11," *New Testament Studies* 5 (1958–59): 45–47.

70. Ibid., 80. Bauckham allows that Jude's description of Cain and Balaam "...perhaps also hinted at their judgment." In light of his broader purpose, however, it seems that Jude emphasizes God's judgment against these individuals to demonstrate that judgment belongs to God alone.

71. Wayne Meeks, "Social Functions of Apocalyptic Language in Pauline Christianity," in *Apocalypticism in the Mediterranean World and the Near East*, ed. David Hellholm (Tübingen: J. C. B. Mohr [Paul Siebeck], 1983), 689. Meeks lists the following: (1) secrets are revealed to the author or prophet; (2) these secrets deal with the soon to be transformation from "this age" to the "age to come"; (3) judgment is a central theme; (4) the universe is characterized by cosmic, temporal, and social duality.

72. Ibid., 700. After examining 1 Thessalonians, Galatians, and 1 Corinthians, Meeks lists the following social functions of apocalyptic language in Pauline Christianity: (1) To emphasize and legitimate boundaries between the Christian groups and the larger society; (2) To enhance internal cohesion and solidarity; (3) To provide sanctions for normative behavior; (4) To warrant innovations over against Jewish norms and structures from which Christianity emerged; (5) To

resist, on the other hand, deviant behavior that led to disruption of the Christian community; (6) To legitimate the leadership of Paul and his associates against challenges; (7) To justify radical interpretation of scripture and tradition.

73. See, however, David W. Kruk, "'Each Will Bear His Own Burden': Paul's Creative Use of an Apocalyptic Motif," *New Testament Studies* 40 (1994): 289–297; Douglas Alan Low, "Apocalyptic Motivation in Pauline Paraenesis" (Ph.D. diss. The Southern Baptist Theological Seminary, 1988).

74. Meeks, "The Social Function of Apocalyptic," 697.

75. Rowland, *The Open Heaven*, 2.

76. Ibid.

77. Ibid., 11. Emphasis added.

78. Cf. Ellis, "Prophecy and Hermeneutic in Jude" and Bauckham, *Jude, 2 Peter*.

79. Verses 22–23 present a significant textual problem. C. D. Osburn, "The Text of Jude 22–23," *Zeitschrift für die neutestamentliche Wissenschaft* 63 (1972): 139, argues that this is "...one of the most corrupt passages in New Testament literature." Metzger, *A Textual Commentary*, 727, outlines the texts that have been transmitted. Bauckham, *Jude, 2 Peter*, 108–111, provides a cogent description of the various texts and possible translations. The primary textual problem requires a determination about a "three-clause" text, or a "two-clause" text. Bauckham favors the two-clause text on "... the grounds of it attestation [p^{72} supported by B, C, K, L, P, S, and Clement of Alexandria *Strom.* 6.8.65], its suitability to the context in Jude, and because it is possible to explain the various longer readings as expansions and adaptations" (110).

80. Bauckham, *Jude, 2 Peter*, 20. Bauckham cites K. Berger, "Apostelbrief und apostolische Rede," *Zeitschrift für die neutestamentliche Wissenschaft* 65 (1974): 191–201. Bauckham refers to examples which wish peace to recipients, but he cites only one example of an extant Jewish letter where the wish for mercy is added to the salutation, *2 Apoc. Bar.* 78:2: "Mercy and peace be with you."

81. Ibid. Bauckham cites Num 6:25–26; Tob 7:12; *1 Enoch* 5:6; 2 Sam 2:6; 15:20; Ps 33:22.

82. The optative πληθυνθείη is rare in the NT (1 Pet 1:2; 2 P 1:2). Bauckham accepts Berger's contention that the word "...derives from blessings formulae... and is found in both Jewish and early Christian letter salutations" (Ibid).

83. Bauckham, *Jude, 2 Peter*, 20.

84. Stassen, "Critical Variables in Christian Social Ethics," 67. Emphasis added.

85. Bauckham, *Jude, 2 Peter*, 117. For Bauckham, verses 20–23 contain Jude's appeal, "...the main purpose of his letter, which is to give his readers positive instructions about how, in the situation in which they find themselves, they are to 'carry on the fight for the faith' (v. 3)."

86. Stassen, "Critical Variables," 65. Stassen cites James Gustafson, *Christ and the Moral Life* (New York: Harper & Row, 1968), 118–119, who outlines five "...divergent understandings of the Christian life" stemming from the understanding of the relationship between justification and sanctification: (1) emphasis on justification alone which "leads to a Christianity in which Christ is not the norm for life;" (2) emphasis on sanctification which ignores the "need for legal and ecclesiastical provisions for correcting Christians who are sinful;" (3) emphasis on Jesus Christ as *teacher*, (4) emphasis on Jesus Christ as *pattern*; (5) emphasis on Jesus Christ as *Lord* (Ibid., 66–67).

87. This understanding of "faith" is critical for Jude. It is the social distinctive which sets apart the community of believers. It relates primarily to Jude's loyalties, interests, and trusts (see below, 185); however, Jude's faith dimension stems from his ground of meaning beliefs about the channel and power to do ethics. See also, Heiligenthal, "Die Weisheitsschrift aus der Kairoer Geniza und der Judasbrief," 358; Wright, *Climax of the Covenant*, 3.

88. Stassen, "Critical Variables," 67. See Gustafson, *Christ and the Moral Life*, 14; 32–34; 44–45.

89. Ibid., 111–112. ἐποιδοδομοῦντες... προσευχόμενοι... τηρήσατε... προσδεχόμενοι: The three participles dependent on the single imperative can explain "...the construction as normal Greek usage." Bauckham cites the use of participles with the imperative in NT parenesis (Rom 12:9–19; Eph 4:2–3; Col 3:16–17; Heb 13:5; 1 Pet 2:18; 3:1, 7–9; 4:7–10) where the participle carries the force of the imperative and suggests that this may be Jude's intention. Bauckham demonstrates that these four admonitions stem from "traditional catechetical material" following two basic patterns: (1) faith, love, hope; (2) Holy Spirit, God, Christ (112).

90. See Heiligenthal, "Die Weisheitschrift der Kairoer Geniza und der Judasbrief," 357. The "building" metaphor is common in the NT: Matt 16:18; Acts 9:31; 15:16; 20:32; 1 Pet 2:5; Rom 14:19; 15:2, 20; 1 Cor 3:9–15; 8:1; 10:23; 14:3–5, 12, 17, 26; 2 Cor 10:8; 12:19; 13:10; Gal 2:18; Eph 2:18; 2:20–22; 4:12, 16; Col 2:7; 1 Thess 5:11. While most of the occurrences come from Paul's writings, Bauckham, *Jude, 2 Peter*, 112, argues that "Paul himself will have been dependent on common Christian usage, and it is probable that exhortations to 'build up' the community or to 'edify' one's Christian brother, both in Paul and elsewhere..., go back to traditional catechetical material."

91. Bauckham, *Jude, 2 Peter*, 112–113.

92. Neyrey, *Jude, 2 Peter*, 90. Neyrey translates τῇ ἁγιωτάτῃ ὑμῶν πίστει as "by the most sacred faithfulness," and argues that Jude exhorts the community to practice certain virtues which "denote constancy and fidelity," and which offer honor and loyalty to God as patron.

93. Ibid.

94. Ibid. Neyrey continues: "Similarly, the true Spirit inspires the faithful in 1 John to confess the orthodox formula (4:2). Thus because of its context, 'praying in the Spirit' has to do with honoring God, not denying the Lord, and with acclaiming authority, not flouting it."

95. Ibid., 91.

96. Ibid. Cf. Bauckham, *Jude, 2 Peter*, 113–114, who distinguishes between the subjective genitive θεοῦ (God's love for you), and the objective genitive (your love for God). Bauckham holds to the former and like Neyrey argues that "…Jude probably means that God's love for Christians (v. 1) requires an appropriate response."

97. Bauckham, *Jude, 2 Peter*, 114. See also Neyrey, *Jude, 2 Peter*, 91. Both Bauckham and Neyrey cite the tradition in 2 Macc. 2:7 and the "waiting" of righteous individuals (Mark 15:43; Luke 2:25, 38).

98. Ibid.

99. Stassen, "Critical Variables," 67.

Notes for Chapter Five

1. N. T. Wright, *Climax of the Covenant*, 2. See also, Heiligenthal, "Die Weisheitsschrift aus der Kairoer Geniza und der Judasbrief," 358.

2. Ibid., 3. Wright argues that: "On the one hand, the boundary-marker must be faith in Christ, and those whose behavior or affirmations show that they do not have such faith are to be regarded as outside. On the other hand, the boundary-marker is faith in Christ and *not* Jewish race, with its badges or circumcision, kosher laws, sabbath observance and, in and through all, the possession of, or attempts to keep, Torah, so that racial background is irrelevant to membership in the people of God. Paul's theology thus has, if you like, a sociological cutting edge."

3. Ibid.

4. The understanding of πίστις conforms to the more concrete classical definition "...the 'guarantee' which creates the possibility of trust... πίστις is the 'oath of fidelity,' the 'pledge of faithfulness,'... this leads on one side to the sense of 'certainty,' 'trustworthiness,' on the other to that of 'means of proof,' 'proof.'" Rudolph Bultmann, "πίστις," in *Theological Dictionary of the New Testament*, ed. Gerhard Friedrich, trans. Geoffrey W. Bromiley, vol. 6 (Grand Rapids: Wm. B. Eerdmans, 1968), 177.

5. See Bauckham, *Jude and the Relatives of Jesus*, chapter five, "Jude's Christology."

6. Ibid., 282. Bauckham convincingly states the case for the common use of each of these titles within the milieu of Palestinian Jewish Christianity. Of Jude's use of Χριστός, Bauckham states: "Among other New Testament authors, this frequency (relative to length) [six times in twenty-five verses] is matched and sometimes surpassed only by Paul" (ibid., 285).

7. On demonstrations of discipleship (sanctification) as yielding allegiance to the lordship of Jesus Christ, see above, 74-76.

8. Most commentators feel this phrase refers to a particular slander against angels. See Bauckham, *Jude, 2 Peter*, 57–59, who outlines five possible interpretations and concludes that the δόξαι should be equated with the angels as "givers and guardians of the law of Moses whom the false teachers slandered and, we may add, the angels as guardians of the created order" (58). Neyrey, *Jude, 2 Peter*, is tempted "...to interpret this as a reference to the illustrious members of the church of Jude," but he too suspects that it refers to "angels of the court of God of glory" (69).

9. Attempts to identify a specific heresy are interesting, but speculative at best. (See the discussion in chapter three.) Jude's emphasis on behavior is clear, and it seems best to interpret the ethical admonitions in the letter as a response to behavioral problems rather than to doctrinal positions.

10. Most scholars hold that Jude does not admonish mercy towards the troublemakers delineated in verses 5–19. For example, Neyrey, *Jude, 2 Peter*, 91, states: "Jude surely does not refer here to the scoffers; all along he has marked them for judgment and destruction (vv 4, 9, 13, 14–15)." This conclusion assumes that Jude condemns a false teaching rather than incorrect behavior. Neyrey posits "scoffers" who are outside the boundary of the community; however, Jude's admonition is directed precisely to those in the community who deny the lordship of Christ.

11. Cf. Charles, *Literary Strategy in the Epistle of Jude*; Ellis, *Prophecy and Hermeneutic*; and Watson, *Invention, Arrangement and Style*. (See above, 44–48.)

12. Stassen, "Critical Variables," 61.

13. Vögtle, *Der Judasbrief*, 114.

Bibliography

Adler, William. "Enoch in Early Christian Literature." In *SBL 1978 Seminar Papers*, vol. 1, ed. P. J. Achtemeier, 271–275. Missoula, Montana: Scholars Press, 1978.

Aiken, Henry David. *Reason and Conduct*. New York: Knopf, 1962.

Alexander, Paul J. *The Byzantine Apocalyptic Tradition*. Berkeley: University of California Press, 1985.

Argyle, A. W. "Greek among the Jews of Palestine in New Testament Times." *New Testament Studies* 20 (1973–74): 87–89.

Arichea, Daniel C., and Howard A. Hatton. *A Handbook on The Letter from Jude and the Second Letter from Peter*. New York: United Bible Societies, 1993.

Attridge, Harold W. "Greek and Latin Apocalypses." *Semeia* 14 (1979): 159–186.

Aune, David E. "The Significance of the Delay of the Parousia for Early Christianity." In *Current Issues in Biblical and Patristic Interpretation: Studies in Honor of Merrill C. Tenney*, ed. Gerald F. Hawthorne, 87–109. Grand Rapids: Wm. B. Eerdmans, 1975.

Axtell, Richard D. "Ghandian Developmental Ethics as a Constructive Response to the Modernization of Dependency Debate." Ph.D. diss., The Southern Baptist Theological Seminary, 1992.

Barker, Margaret. *The Great Angel: A Study of Israel's Second God*. London: SPCK, 1992.

_____. *The Lost Prophet: The Book of Enoch and Its Influence on Chrstianity*. London: SPCK, 1988.

_____. *The Older Testament*. London: SPCK, 1987.

Barnett, Albert E. "The Epistle of Jude." In *The Interpreter's Bible*, vol. 12. New York: Abingdon Press, 1957.

Barns, Thomas. "The Epistle of St. Jude: A Study in the Marcosian Heresy." *Journal of Theological Studies* 6 (1905): 391–411.

Bartlett, James V. *The Apostolic Age: Its Life, Doctrine, Worship and Polity*. Edinburgh: T & T Clark, 1900.

Bauckham, Richard J. "The Delay of the Parousia." *Tyndale Bulletin* 31 (1980): 3–36.

_____. "James, 1 and 2 Peter, Jude." In It is Written: Scripture Citing Scripture: Essays In Honour of Barnabas Lindars SSF, ed. D. A. Carson and H. G. M. Williamson, 303–317. Cambridge: Cambridge University Press, 1988.

_____. *Jude, 2 Peter*. Word Biblical Commentary, vol. 50. Waco: Word Books, 1983.

_____. *Jude and the Relatives of Jesus*. Edinburgh: T & T Clark, 1990.

_____. "The Letter of Jude: An Account of Research." In *Aufstieg und Niedergang der römischen Welt*, vol. 2/25/5, ed. W. Hasse, 3791–3826. Berlin/New York: de Gruyter, 1988.

_____. "The Liber Antiquitatum Biblicarum of Pseudo-Philo and the Gospels as 'Midrash'." In *Gospel Perspectives III: Studies in Midrash and Historiography*, ed. R. T. France and David Wenham, 33–76. Sheffield: JSOT Press, 1983.

_____. "A Note on a Problem in the Greek Version of I Enoch i.9." *Journal of Theological Studies* 32 (1981): 136–138.

_____. "Pseudo-Apostolic Letters." *Journal of Biblical Literature* 107 (1988): 469–494.

_____. "The Son of Man: 'A Man in My Position' or 'Someone'?" *Journal for the Study of the New Testament* 23 (1985): 22–33.

_____. "2 Peter: An Account of Research." In *Aufstieg und Niedergang der römischen Welt*, vol. 2/25/5, ed. W. Hasse, 3713–3752. Berlin/New York: de Gruyter, 1988.

Bauer, Walter., William F. Arndt, and F. Wilbur Gingrich. *A Greek-English Lexicon of the New Testament and Other Early Christian Literature*. 4th ed. Chicago: University of Chicago Press, 1952.

Beardslee, William A. "New Testament Apocalyptic in Recent Interpretation." *Interpretation* 25 (1971): 419–435.

Beasley-Murray, George R. "The Eschatological Discourse of Jesus." *Review and Expositor* 57 (1960): 153–166.

_____. "Eschatology in the Gospel of Mark." *Southwestern Journal of Theology* 21 (1978): 37–53.

_____. *The General Epistles: James, 1 Peter, Jude, 2 Peter*. New York: Abingdon Press, 1965.

_____. "The Interpretation of Daniel 7." *Catholic Biblical Quarterly* 45 (1983): 44–58.

_____. *Jesus and the Kingdom of God*. Grand Rapids: Wm. B. Eerdmans, 1986.

Becker, J. C. "Jude, Letter of." In *The Interpreter's Dictionary of the Bible*, ed. G. A. Buttrick, vol. 2, 1009–1011. New York: Abingdon Press, 1962.

Beckwith, Roger T. *The Old Testament Canon of the New Testament Church and its Background in Early Judaism*. London: SPCK, 1985.

Berger, K. "Apostelbrief und apostolische Rede." *Zeitschrift für die neutestamentliche Wissenschaft* 65 (1974): 191–201.

Berkhof, Hendrikus. *Christian Faith: An Introduction to the Study of Faith*. Translated by Sierd Wostra. Grand Rapids: Wm. B. Eerdmans, 1986.

Betz, Otto. "The Eschatological Interpretation of the Sinai-Tradition in Qumran and in the New Testament." *Revue de Qumran* 6 (1967): 89–107.

Bieder, Werner. "Judas 22f.: Οὕς δὲ ἐᾶτε ἐν φόβω." *Theologische Zeitschrift* 6 (1950):75–77.

Bigg, Charles. *A Critical and Exegetical Commentary on the Epistles of St. Peter and St. Jude*. ICC. Endinburgh: T & T Clark, 1901.

Black, Matthew. *An Aramaic Approach to the Gospels and Acts*. Oxford: Clarendon Press, 1967.

_____. "Aramaic Barnasha and the 'Son of Man'." *Expository Times* 95 (1983–84): 200–206.

_____. *The Book of Enoch or I Enoch: A New English Studies Edition*. SVTP 7. Leiden: Brill, 1985.

_____. "The Christological Use of the Old Testament in the New Testament." *New Testament Studies* 18 (1972): 1–14.

_____. "Critical and Exegetical Notes on Three New Testament Texts, Hebrews 11:2, Jude 5, James 1:27." In *Apophoreta: Festschrift für Ernst Haenchen.* BZNW 30, 39–45. Berlin: A. Töpelmann, 1964.

_____. "The Eschatology of the Similitudes of Enoch." *Journal of Theological Studies* n.s. 3 (1978): 4–12.

_____. "The Maranatha Invocation and Jude 14, 15 (1 Enoch 1:9)." In *Christ and Spirit in the New Testament,C. F. D. Moule Festschrift,* ed. B. Lindars, and S.S. Smalley, 189–196. Cambridge: Cambridge University Press, 1973.

_____. "The Theological Appropriation of the Old Testament by the New Testament." *Scottish Journal of Theology* 39 (1986): 1–17.

Boobyer, G. H. "Jude." In *Peake's Commentary on the Bible,* edited by Matthew Black and H. H. Rowley. London: Nelson, 1963.

_____. "The Verbs in Jude 11." *New Testament Studies* 5 (1958–59): 45–47.

Brown, Raymond E. "Not Jewish Christianity and Gentile Christianity but Types of Jewish/Gentile Christianity." *Catholic Biblical Quarterly* 45 (1983): 74–79.

Bruce, F. F. "Jude, Epistle of." In *The Illustrated Bible Dictionary,* rev., vol. 2, ed. N. Hillyer, 831–832. Leicester: Intervarsity Press, 1980.

_____. *Men and Movements in the Primitive Church: Studies in Early Non-Pauline Christianity.* Exeter: Paternoster, 1979.

_____. "A Reappraisal of Jewish Apocalyptic Literature." *Review and Expositor* 72 (1975): 305–315.

_____. *This is That: The New Testament Development of Some Old Testament Themes.* Exeter: Paternoster, 1968.

Bultmann, Rudolf. "πίστις". *Theological Dictionary of the New Testament,* vol. 6. Ed. Gerhard Friedrich. Translated by Geoffrey W. Bromiley. Grand Rapids: Wm. B. Eerdmans, 1968.

Burkitt, F. C. "Moses, Assumption of." In *A Dictionary of the Bible,* vol. 3, ed. James Hastings, 448–450. Edinburgh: T & T Clark, 1900.

Calvin, John. *Commentaries on The Catholic Epistles.* Translated John Owen. Grand Rapids: Wm. B. Eerdmans, 1948.

Cantinat, Jean. "The Catholic Epistles." In *Introduction to the New Testament,* eds.A. Robert and A. Feuillet. New York: Desclee, 1965.

_____. *Les épîtres de Saint Jacques et de Saint Jude,* SB. Paris: Gabalda, 1973.

Carlson, D. C. "Vengence and Angelic Mediation in The Testament of Moses 9 and 10." *Journal of Biblical Literature* 101 (1982): 55–58.

Carmignac, Jean. "Le document de Qumran sur Melkisédeq." *Revue de Qumran* 7 (1969–71): 343–378.

Carrington, Phillip. *The Early Christian Church,* vol. 1. Cambridge: Cambridge University Press, 1957.

Casey, P. Maurice. "Aramaic Idiom and Son of Man Sayings." *Expository Times* 96 (1984–85): 233–236.

_____. "General, Generic, and Indefinite: The Use of the Term 'Son of Man' in Aramaic Sources and in the Teachings of Jesus." *Journal for the Study of the New Testament* 29 (1987): 21–56.

_____. "The Jackals and the Son of Man." *Journal for the Study of the New Testament* 23 (1985): 3–22.

_____. "Method in Our Madness, and Madness in Their Methods: Some Approaches to the Son of Man Problem in Recent Scholarship." *Journal for the Study of the New Testament* 42 (1991): 17–43.

_____. "The Son of Man Problem." *Zeitschrift für die neutestamentliche Wissenschaft* 67 (1976): 147–54.

Cavallin, H. C. C. "The False Teachers of 2 Pt as Pseudo-Prophets." *Novum Testamentum* 21 (1979): 263–270.

Chaine, J. *Les épîtres catholiques: La seconde épître de Saint Pierre, les épîtres de Saint Jean, l'épîtres de Saint Jude*, EBib 27. Paris: Gabalda, 1939.

Charles, J. Daryl. *Literary Strategy in the Epistle of Jude*. Scranton: University of Scranton Press, 1993.

_____. "'Those' and 'these': The Use of the OT in the Epistle of Jude." *Journal for the Study of the New Testament* 38 (1990): 109–124.

_____. "The Use of Traditional Material in the Epistle of Jude." *Bulletin of Biblical Research* 4 (1994):1–14.

Charles, Robert H. *The Apocrypha and Pseudepigrapha of the Old Testament in English*, vol. 2. Oxford: Clarendon Press, 1913.

_____. *The Assumption of Moses*. London: A & C Black, 1897.

_____. *The Book of Enoch*. Oxford: Clarendon Press, 1893.

Charlesworth, James H. *The Pseudepigrapha and Modern Research With Supplement*. SBL Septuagint and Cognate Studies 7. Chico, CA: Scholars Press, 1981.

_____. "Research on the Historical Jesus Today: Jesus and the Pseudepigrapha, Dead Sea Scrolls, Nag Hammadi Codices, Josephus, and Archeology." *Princeton Seminary Bulletin* 6 (1985): 98–115.

_____, ed. *The Old Testament Pseudepigrapha*, vol. 1. Garden City, NY: Doubleday and Co., 1983.

Chase, Frederic H. "Jude, Epistle of." In *A Dictionary of the Bible*, vol. 2, ed. James Hastings, 799–806. Edinburgh: T & T Clark, 1899.

Chazon, E. Glickler. "Moses' Struggle for His Soul: A Prototype for the *Apocalypse of Abraham*, the *Greek Apocalypse of Ezra*, and the *Apocalypse of Sedrach*." *Second Century* 5 (1985–86): 151–164.

Chester, Andrew, and Ralph Martin. *The Theology of the Letters of James, Peter, and Jude*. New Testament Theology. Ed. J. D. G. Dunn. Cambridge: Cambridge University Press, 1994.

Church, Christopher L. "A Forschungsgeschichte on the Literary Character of the Epistle of James." Ph.D diss., The Southern Baptist Theological Seminary, 1990.

Cladder, H. J. "Strophical Structure in St. Jude's Epistle." *Journal of Theological Studies* 5 (1904): 589–601.

Clark, Kenneth W. "Worship in the Jerusalem Temple after AD 70." *New Testament Studies* 6 (1969/1970): 269–280.

Coke, Paul T. "The Angels of the Son of Man." In *Probleme der Forschung*, ed. Albert Fuchs. Munich: Herold Wren, 1978.

Collins, Adelya Yarbro. "Daniel 7 and the Historical Jesus." In *Of Scribes and Scrolls*. Ed. Harold W. Attridge, John J. Collins, and Thomas H. Tobin S. J. New York: University Press of America, 1990.

_____. "Daniel 7 and Jesus." *Journal of Theology UTS* 93 (1989): 5–19.

_____. "The Early Christian Apocalypses." *Semeia* 14 (1979): 61–122.

_____. "The Origins of the Designation Jesus as Son of Man." *Harvard Theological Review* 80 (1987):391–407.

Collins, John J., ed. "Apocalypse: The Morphology of a Genre." *Semeia* 14 (1979).

_____. "Apocalyptic Eschatology as the Transcendence of Death." *Catholic Biblical Quarterly* 36 (1974): 21–43.

_____. *The Apocalyptic Imagination: An Introduction to the Jewish Matrix of Christianity*. New York: Crossroad, 1984.

_____. "The Heavenly Representative: The 'Son of Man' in the Similitudes of Enoch." In *Ideal Figures in Ancient Judaism*, ed. John J. Collins and George W. E. Nickelsburg. Chico, CA: Scholars Press, 1980.

_____. "Introduction: Towards the Morphology of a Genre." *Semeia* 14 (1979): 1–20.

_____. "The Jewish Apocalypses." *Semeia* 14 (1979): 21–60.

_____. "Persian Apocalypses." *Semeia* 14 (1979): 207–217.

_____. "The Symbolism of Transcendence in Jewish Apocalyptic." *Biblical Research* 19 (1974): 1–18.

_____. "Testaments." In M. E. Stone, *Jewish Writings of the Second Temple Period*. CRINT 2/2. Philadelphia: Fortress Press, 1984.

Colpe, Carsten. "ὁ υἱὸς τοῦ ἀνθρώπου." *Theological Dictionary of the New Testament*, vol. 8. Ed. Gerhard Kittel. Translated by G. W. Bromiley. Grand Rapids: Wm. B. Eerdmans, 1964.

Cortis, J. B., and F. M. Gatti. "The Son of Man or the Son of Adam." *Biblica* 49 (1968): 457–502.

Cranfield, C. E. B. *I & II Peter and Jude*. TBC. London: SCM Press, 1960.

Cross, F. M. "Exile and Apocalyptic." In *Canaanite Myth and Hebrew Epic: Essays in the History of the Religion of Israel*, 291–346. Cambridge, MA: Harvard University, 1973.

_____. "New Directions in the Study of Apocalyptic." *Journal for Theology and the Church* 6 (1969): 157–165.

Dalton, William J. "Jude." In *A New Catholic Commentary on Holy Scripture*, ed. R. C. Fuller, L. Johnston and C. Kearns, 1263–1265. London: Nelson, 1969.

Daniel, Constantin. "La mention des Esséniens dans le texte grec de l'épître de S. Jude." *Le Muséon* 81 (1968): 503–521.

Danker, Frederick W. "Jude, Epistle of." In *The International Standard Bible Encyclopedia*, vol. 2, ed. G. W. Bromiley, 1153–1155. Grand Rapids: Wm. B. Eerdmans, 1982.

Davidson, Maxwell. *Angels at Qumran: A Comparitive Study of 1 Enoch 1–36, 72–108, and Sectarian Writings from Qumran.* JSPSS 11. Sheffield: JSOT Press, 1992.

Davis, Phillip G. "The Mystic Enoch: New Light on Early Christology." *Studies in Religion/Science* 13 (1984): 335–343.

DeJonge, Marinus. *Jewish Eschatology, Early Christian Christology and the Testament of the Twelve Patriarchs.* Leiden: E.J. Brill, 1991.

_____. "The Role of Intermediaries in God's Final Intervention in the Future According to the Qumran Scrolls." In *Jewish Eschatology, Early Christian Christology and the Testament of the Twelve Patriarchs.* Leiden: E.J. Brill, 1991.

_____., ed. *Outside the Old Testament.* Cambridge: Cambridge University Press, 1985.

Delcor, Mathias. *Le Testament d'Abraham.* SVTP, 2. Leiden: Brill, 1973.

Denis, Albert-Marie. *Concordance Grecque des Pseudépigraphes D'ancien Testament.* Universite Catholique de Louvain. Institut Orientallste. Louvain la-Neu, 1987.

Desjardins, Michel. "The Portrayal of the Dissidents in 2 Peter and Jude: Does it Tell Us More about the 'Godly' than the 'Ungodly'?" *Journal for the Study of the New Testament* 30 (1987): 89–102.

Donahue, John R. "Recent Studies on the Origin of 'Son of Man' in the Gospels." *Catholic Biblical Quarterly* 48 (1986): 484–498.

Dubarle, A.-M. "'Le péché des anges dans l'épître de Jude." In *Memorial J. Chaine.* Lyons: Facultés Catholiques, 1950.

Dunn, James D. G. *Unity and Diversity in the New Testament: An Inquiry into the Character of Earliest Christianity.* London: SCM Press, 1980.

Durnett, Walter M. "The Hermeneutics of Jude and 2 Peter: The Use of Ancient Jewish Traditions." *Journal of the Evangelical Theological Society* 31 (1988): 287–292.

Efird, James M. *Revelation for Today: An Apocalyptic Approach.* Nashville: Abingdon Press, 1989.

Elliot, John H. "I–II Peter/Jude." *Augsburg Commentary on the New Testament.* Minneapolis: Augsburg Publishing House, 1982.

_____. "Man and the Son of Man in the Gospel According to Mark." In *Humane Gesellschaft.* Ed. Trutz Rentorff and Arthur Rich. Zurich: Zwingli-Verlag, 1970.

Ellis, E. Earle. *Prophecy and Hermeneutic in Early Christianity.* Tübingen: Mohr, 1978.

Erasmus. *Collected Works of Erasmus,* 86 vols. Ed. Robert D. Sider. Toronto: University of Toronto Press, 1993.

Everding, H. Edward, and Dana W. Wilbanks. *Decision-Making and the Bible.* Valley Forge: Judson Press, 1975.

Fallon, Francis. "The Gnostic Apocalypses." *Semeia* 14 (1979): 123–158.

Farkasfalvy, Denis. "The Ecclesial Setting of Pseudepigraphy in Second Peter and Its Role in the Formation of the Canon." *The Second Century* 5 (1985): 3–29.

Feldman, Louis. "Hengel's Judaism and Hellenism in Retrospect." *Journal of Biblical Literature* 96 (Spring 1977): 371–382.

_____. "How Much Hellenism In Jewish Palestine?" *Hebrew Union College Annual* 57 (1986): 83–111.

Fitzmyer, Joseph A. "Another View of the 'Son of Man' Debate." *Journal for the Study of the New Testament* 4 (1979): 58–68.

_____. "The Languages of Palestine in the First Century A.D." In *A Wandering Aramaean: Collected Aramaic Essays*, SBLMS 25. Missoula, MT: Scholars Press, 1979.

_____. "The New Testament title 'Son of Man' Philologically Considered." In *A Wandering Aramaean: Collected Aramaic Essays*, SBLMS 25. Missoula, MT: Scholars Press, 1979.

_____. "The Semitic Background of the New Testament Kyrios-Title." In *A Wandering Aramaean: Collected Aramaic Essays*, SBLMS 25. Missoula, MT: Scholars Press, 1979.

_____. "The Use of Explicit Old Testament Quotations in Qumran Literature and in the New Testament." *New Testament Studies* 7 (1960/1961): 297–333.

Fornburg, Tord. *An Early Church in a Pluralistic Society: A Study of 2 Peter.* ConB. NT. 9. Lund: C. W. K. Gleerup, 1977.

Fossum, Jarl. "Kyrios Jesus as the Angel of the Lord in Jude 5–7." *New Testament Studies* 33 (1987): 226–243.

Fuchs, E., and Reymond, P. *La deuxième épître de Saint Pierre; L'Épître de Saint Jude.* Neuchâtel: Delachaux et Niestlé, 1980.

Glasson, T. Francis. *Greek Influence in Jewish Eschatology.* London: SPCK, 1961.

Gloag, Paton J. *Introduction to the Catholic Epistles.* Edinburgh: T & T Clark, 1987.

Gnilka, Joachim. "Apokalyptik und Ethik." In *Neues Testament und Ethik: für Rudolf Schnackenburg*, ed. Helmut Merklein, 464–481. Freiburg, Basel, Wien: Herder, 1989.

Goodspeed, Edgar J. *Introduction to the New Testament.* Chicago: University of Chicago Press, 1937.

Grant, Robert M., and David Tracy. *A Short History of the Interpretation of the Bible.* 2nd ed. Philadelphia: Fortress Press, 1984.

Green, Edward M.B. *The Second Epistle General of Peter and the General Epistle of Jude.* London: Intervarsity Press, 1968.

Grenz, Stanley. *Theology for the Community of God.* Nashville: Broadman & Holmann, 1994.

Gruenwald, Ithamar. *From Apocalypticism to Gnosticism: Studies in Apocalypticism, Merkavah Mysticism, and Gnosticism.* Beitrage zur Erforschung des Alten Testaments und des antiken Judentums, Bdr. 14. Frankfurt am Main: Peter Lang, 1988.

Grundmann, Walter. *Der Brief des Judas und der zweite brief des Petrus.* THKNT 15. Berlin: Evangelische Verlagsanstalt, 1974.

Gunther, John J. "The Alexandrian Epistle of Jude." *New Testament Studies* 30 (1984): 549–562.

_____. *St. Paul's Opponents and Their Background: A Study of Apocalyptic and Jewish Sectarian Teachings.* Novum Testamentum, Supplements 35. Leiden: Brill, 1973.

Guthrie, Donald. *Hebrews to Revelation, New Testament Introduction.* London: Tyndale Press, 1964.

_____. *New Testament Introduction.* Downers Grove, IL: Intervarsity Press, 1970.

Hafemann, Scott J. "Moses in the Apocrypha and Pseudepigrapha: A Survey." *Journal for the Study of Pseudepigrapha* 7 (1990): 79–104.

Hamerton-Kelly, R. "The Temple and the Origins of Jewish Apocalyptic." *Vetus Testamentum* 20 (1970): 1–15.

Hanson, Paul D. "Apocalypse, Genre," and "Apocalypticism." *International Dictionary of the Bible, Supp.*, 27–34. Nashville: Abingdon, 1976.

_____. *The Dawn of Apocalyptic*. Philadelphia: Fortress, 1975.

_____. "Jewish Apocalyptic Against its Near Eastern Environment." *Revue Biblique* 78 (1971): 31–58.

_____. *Old Testament Apocalyptic*. Nashville: Abingdon Press, 1987.

_____. "Old Testament Apocalyptic Reexamined." *Interpretation* 25 (1971): 454–479.

_____. *The People Called: The Growth of Community in the Bible*. San Francisco: Harper and Row, 1987.

_____., ed. *Visionaries and Their Apocalypses*. Issues in Religion and Theology 4. Philadelphia: Fortress Press, 1983.

Hare, Douglas R. A. *The Son of Man Tradition*. Minneapolis: Fortress Press, 1990.

Harnack, Adolf. *Geschichte Der Altchristlichen Literatur bis Eusebius*, II/1. Leipzig: J.C. Hinrichs Verlag, 1958.

_____. *The Mission and Expansion of Christianity in the First Three Centuries*, vol. 2. Translated by J. Moffatt. London: Williams and Northgate, 1908.

_____. *The Origin of the New Testament*. Translated by J. R. Wilkinson. London: Williams and Northgate, 1925.

Hartman, Lars. *Asking for Meaning: A Study of 1 Enoch 1–5*. Continectanea Biblica, New Testament Series 12. Uppsala: C. W. K. Gleerup, 1979.

_____. "The Functions of Some So-Called Apocalyptic Timetables." *New Testament Studies* 22 (1975): 1–14.

_____. *Prophecy Interpreted: The Formation of Some Jewish Apocalyptic Texts and of the Eschatological Discourse Mark 13 Par.* Coniectanea Biblica, NT Series 1. Lund: C. W. K. Gleerup, 1966.

Heiligenthal, Roman. "Der Judasbrief: Aspekte der Forschung in den letzten Jahrzehnten." *Theologische Rundschau* 51 (1986): 117–129.

_____. "Die Weisheitsschrift aus der Kairoer Geniza und der Judasbrief. Ein Vergleich zwischen einer umstrittenen jüdischen und einer judenchristlichen Schrift." *Zeitschrift für Religions- und Geistesgeschichte* 44 (1992): 356–361.

_____. *Zwischen Henoch und Paulus. Studien zum theologiegeschichtlichen Ort des Judasbriefes*. TANZ 6 Tübingen: Francke, 1992.

Hellholm, David, ed. *Apocalypticism in the Mediterranean World and the Near East: Proceedings of the International Colloquium on Apocalypticism Aug. 12–17, 1979*. Tübingen: Mohr, 1983.

Hengel, Martin. *The 'Hellenization' of Judaea in the First Century after Christ*. London: SCM Press, 1989.

_____. *Judaism and Hellenism*, vols. 1 & 2. Minneapolis: Fortress Press, 1974.

Hiebert, D. Edmond. *Second Peter and Jude: An Expositional Commentary.* Greenville, SC: Unusual Publications, 1989.

Higgins, Angus J. B. *Jesus and the Son of Man.* Philadelphia: Fortress Press, 1964.

Himmelfarb, Martha. *Tours of Hell: An Apocalyptic Form in Jewish and Christian Literature.* Philadelphia: University of Philadelphia Press, 1983.

Hindley, J. C. "Towards a Date for the Similitudes of Enoch: An Historical Approach." *New Testament Studies* 14 (1968): 551–565.

Hollander, H. W., and Martin DeJonge. *The Testament of the Twelve Patriarchs: A Commentary.* Leiden: E.J. Brill, 1985.

Hooker, Morna. *The Son of Man in Mark.* Montreal: McGill University Press, 1967.

Horburg, W. J. "The Messianic Associations of 'The Son of Man.'" *Journal of Theological Studies* n.s. 36 (1985): 34–55.

James, Montaque R. *The Lost Apocrypha of the Old Testament.* New York: McMillian, 1920.

_____. *The Second Epistle General of Peter and the General Epistle of Jude.* Cambridge Greek Testament for Schools and Colleges. Cambridge: Cambridge University Press, 1912.

Johnson, Elizabeth E. *The Function of Apocalyptic and Wisdom Traditions in Romans 9–11.* SBL Dissertation Series 109. Atlanta: Scholars Press, 1989.

Jülicher, Adolf. *An Introduction to the New Testament.* Translated by J. P. Ward. London: Smith, Elder, & Co., 1904.

Käsemann, Ernst. "An Apologia for Primitive Christian Eschatology." In *Essays on New Testament Themes.* London: SCM Press, 1964.

Kee, Howard Clark. "Christology in Mark's Gospel." *In Judaisms and their Messiahs at the Turn of the Christian Era.* Ed. Jacob Neusner, William Scott Greer, and Ernest S. Frerichs. Cambridge: Cambridge University Press, 1987.

_____. "Messiah and the People of God." In *Understanding the Word.* Ed. Janet T. Butler, Edgar W. Conrad, and Ben Ollenburger. Sheffield: JSOT Press, 1985.

Keil, Carl Friedrich. *Commentar über die Briefe des Petrus and Judas.* Leipzig: Dörffling und Franke, 1883.

Kellet, E. E. "Note on Jude 5." *Expository Times* 15 (1903–4): 381.

Kelly, John N. D. *A Commentary on the Epistles of Peter and Jude.* New York: Harper and Row, Publishers, 1969.

Kim, Seyoon. *"The 'Son of Man'" as the Son of God.* Tübingen: Mohr, 1983.

Kistemaker, Simon J. *New Testament Commentary: Exposition of the Epistle of Peter and the Epistle of Jude.* Grand Rapids: Baker Book House, 1987.

Kittel, Gerhard. "ἄγγελος." In *Theological Dictionary of the New Testament*, vol. 1. Ed. Gerhard Kittel. Translated by Geoffery W. Bromiley. Grand Rapids: Wm. B. Eerdmans, 1974.

Klijn, A. F. J. "Jude 5 to 7." In *The New Testament Age: Essays in Honour of Bo Reicke*, vol. 1, ed. W. C. Weinrich, 237–244. Macon: Mercer University Press, 1984.

Knibb, Michael. *Ethiopic Book of Enoch: A New Edition in the Light of the Aramaic Dead Sea Fragments.* Vols. 1 & 2. Oxford: Clarendon Press, 1978.

_____. "The Ethiopic Book of Enoch." In *Outside the Old Testament*, ed. M. De Jonge, 26–55. Cambridge: Cambridge University Press, 1985.

Koch, Klaus. *The Rediscovery of Apocalyptic: A Polemical Work on a Neglected Area of Biblical Studies and its Damaging Effects on Theology and Philosophy.* Translated by Margaret Kohl. Studies in Biblical Theology, 2nd Series 22. London: SCM, 1972.

Koester, Helmut. *Introduction to the New Testament: Volume 2, History and Literature of Early Christianity.* Philadelphia: Fortress Press, 1982.

Kolenkow, Anitra B. "The Assumption of Moses as a Testament." In *Studies in the Testament of Moses.* Ed. G. W. E. Nickelsburg. SBLSCS 4. Cambridge, MA: SBL. 1973.

_____. "The Genre Testament and Forecasts of the Future in the Hellenistic Jewish Milieu." *Journal for the Study of Judaism* 6 (1975): 57–71.

Kreitzer, Larry J. *Jesus and God in Paul's Eschatology.* Journal for the Study of the New Testament, Supplement 19. Sheffield: JSOT, 1987.

Krodel, Gerhard. "The Letter of Jude." In *Hebrews, James, 1 and 2 Peter, Jude, Revelation*, Pulpit Commentaries, 92–98. Philadelphia: Fortress Press, 1977.

Kruk, David W. "'Each Will Bear His Own Burden': Paul's Creative Use of An Apocalyptic Motif." *New Testament Studies* 40 (1994): 289–297.

Kubo, Sakae. "Jude 22–23: Two-division Form or Three?" In *New Testament Textual Criticism*, Festschrift for B. M. Metzger, ed. E. J. Epp and G. D. Fee, 239–253. Oxford: Clarendon Press, 1981.

Kugelman, Richard. *James and Jude.* New Testament Message 19. Dublin: Veritas, 1980.

Kümmel, Werner G. *Introduction to the New Testament.* Translated by Howard Clark Kee. Nashville: Abingdon Press, 1975.

Laperrousaz, E.-M. *Le Testament de Moïse (généralement appelé "Assomption de Moïse"): Traduction avec introduction et notes, Semitica* 19 (1970): 1–40.

Lawlor, G. L. *Translation and Exposition of the Epistle of Jude.* Nutley, NJ: Presbyterian and Reformed, 1976.

Leaney, Alfred R. C. *The Letters of Peter and Jude.* Cambridge Biblical Commentaries. Cambridge: Cambridge University Press, 1967.

Leivestad, Ragnar. "Exit the Apocalyptic Son of Man." *New Testament Studies* 18 (1972): 243–267.

Levine, Baruch A. "From the Aramaic Enoch Fragments: The Semantics of Cosmography." *Journal of Jewish Studies* 33 (1982): 311–326.

Licht, J. "Taxo or the Apocalyptic Doctrine of Vengeance." *Journal of Jewish Studies* 12 (1961): 95–103.

Lindars, Barnabas. *Jesus Son of Man.* London: SPCK, 1983.

_____. *New Testament Apologetic: The Doctrinal Significance of the Old Testament Quotations.* London: SCM Press, 1961.

_____. "Re-enter the Apocalyptic Son of Man." *New Testament Studies* 22 (1975): 52–72.

_____. "A Response to Richard Bauckham: The Idiomatic Use of Bar Enasha." *Journal for the Study of the New Testament* 23 (1985): 35–41.

Loewenstamm, S. E. "The Death of Moses". In *Studies on the Testament of Abraham*, ed. G. W. E. Nickelsburg, SBLSCS 4, 185–217. Missoula, MT: Scholars Press, 1976.

Loisy, Alfred. *The Origins of the New Testament*. Translated by L. P. Jacks. London: Allen & Unwin, 1950.

Luther, Martin. *Luther's Works*, American Edition, vols. 1–55. Translated by Charles M. Jacobs, Rev. Theodore Bachmann. Philadelphia: Muhlenburg Press, 1960.

Marshall, I.Howard. *The Origins of New Testament Christology*. Downers Grove, IL: Intervarsity Press, 1990.

_____. "Son of Man." In *The Dictionary of Jesus and the Gospels*, ed. Joel B. Green and Scot McKnight. Downers Grove, IL: Intervarsity Press, 1992.

_____. "The Synoptic Son of Man Sayings in Recent Discussion." *New Testament Studies* 12 (1966): 327–351.

Martinez Garcia, Florentino. *Qumran and Apocalyptic: Studies on the Aramaic Texts from Qumran. Studies on the Texts of the Desert of Judah v. 9*. Leiden: Brill, 1992.

Mayor, Joseph B. "The Epistle of St. Jude." In *The Expositors Greek Testament*, vol 5. Ed. W. R. Nicoll. London: Hodder & Stoughton, 1910.

_____. "The Epistle of St. Jude and the Marcosian Heresy." *Journal of Theological Studies* 6 (1905): 569–577.

_____. *The Epistle of St. Jude and the Second Epistle of St. Peter*. London: Macmillan, 1907.

Mearns, Christopher L. "The Son of Man Trajectory and Eschatological Development." *Expository Times* 97 (1985): 8–12.

Meeks, Wayne. "The Social Function of Apocalyptic Language in Pauline Christianity." In *Apocalypticism in the Mediterranean World and the Near East*. Ed. David Hellholm. Tübingen: J. C. B. Mohr (Paul Siebeck), 1983.

Metzger, Bruce. *A Textual Commentary on the New Testament*. New York: United Bible Societies, 1971.

Milik, J. T. *The Books of Enoch*. Oxford: Clarendon, 1976.

_____. "4Q Visions de 'Amram et une citation d'Origène." *Revue Biblique* 79 (1972): 79.

_____. "Problèmes de la Littérature Henochique a la Lumière des Fragments Arameen de Qumran. *Harvard Theological Review* 64 (1971): 233–278.

_____. *Ten Years of Discovery in the Wilderness of Judea. Studies in Biblical Theology*, 26. London, 1959.

Miller, Fergus. "The Background to the Maccabean Revolution; Reflections on Martin Hengel's 'Judaism and Hellenism.'" *Journal of Jewish Studies* 22 (1978): 1–21.

Miller, William R. *Isaiah 24 – 27 and the Origin of Apocalyptic*. Harvard Semitic Monographs 11. Missoula, MT: Scholars Press, 1976.

Minear, Paul S. *New Testament Apocalyptic*. Nashville: Abingdon Press, 1981.

Moffatt, James. *The General Epistles: James, Peter, Judas*. Moffatt New Testament Commentaries. London: Hoddert and Stoughton, 1928.

_____. *An Introduction to the Literature of the New Testament*. Edinburgh: T & T Clark, 1918.

Moloney, Francis J. "The End of the Son of Man?" *Downside Review* 98 (1980): 280–290.

Moule, C. F. D. *An Idiom Book of New Testament Greek.* Cambridge: Cambridge University Press, 1959.

Neusner, Jacob. "Judaism in a Time of Crisis: Four Responses to the Destruction of the Second Temple." *Judaism* 21 (1972): 313–27.

Neyrey, Jerome, H. *2 Peter, Jude.* The Anchor Bible, vol. 37c. New York: Doubleday, 1993.

Nickelsburg, George W. "An Antiochan Date for the Testament of Moses." In *Studies on the Testament Moses*, SBLSCS 4, 33–37. Cambridge, MA: SBL, 1973.

_____. "Apocalyptic and Myth in 1 Enoch 6–11." *Journal of Biblical Literature* 96 (1977): 383–405.

_____. "Enoch, Levi, and Peter: Recipients of Revelation in Upper Galilee." *Journal of Biblical Literature*, 100/4 (1981): 575–600.

_____. *Jewish Literature Between the Bible and the Mishnah.* London: SCM Press, 1981.

Nilson, Robert. "This World and the World to Come: Apocalyptic Religion and the Counterculture." *Encounter* 38 (1977): 117–124.

Oleson, John P. "An Echo of Hesiod's Theogony vv 190–2 in Jude 13." *New Testament Studies* 25 (1979): 492–503.

Osburn, Carroll D. "The Christological Use of I Enoch i.9 in Jude 14,15." *New Testament Studies* 23 (1976–77): 334–341.

_____. "I Enoch 80:2–8 (67:5–7) and Jude 12–13." *Catholic Biblical Quarterly* 47 (1985): 296–303.

_____. "The Text of Jude 5." *Biblica* 62 (1981): 107–115.

_____. "The Text of Jude 22–23." *Zeitschrift für die neutestamentliche Wissenschaft* 63 (1972): 139–144.

Otto, Rudolf. *The Kingdom of God and the Son of Man.* Translated by F. V. Filson and Bertrm L. Woolf. London: Lutterworth Press, 1943.

Patte, Daniel. *Early Jewish Hermeneutic in Palestine.* SBL Dissertation Series 22. Missoula, MT: Scholars Press, 1975.

Paulsen, Henning. *Der Zweite Petrusbrief und der Judasbrief.* Kritisch-exegetischer Kommentar über das Neue Testament. Ed. H. A. W. Meyer. Göttingen: Vandenhoeck & Ruprecht, 1992.

Perrin, Norman. "The Creative Use of the Son of Man Traditions by Mark." *Union Seminary Quarterly Review* 23/24 (1968), 357–365.

_____. *The New Testament: An Introduction.* New York: Harcourt Brace Javanovich, 1974.

Pfleiderer, Otto. *Primitive Christianity: Its Writings and Teaching in Their Historical Connections*, vol. 4. Translated by W. Montgomery. Clifton, NJ: Reference Book Publishers, 1965.

Potter, Ralph. "The Logic of Moral Argument." In *Toward a Discipline of Social Ethics.* Ed. Paul Deats. Boston: Boston University Press, 1972.

_____. "The Structure of Certain American Christian Responses to the Nuclear Dilemma." Ph.D. diss., Harvard University, 1965.

_____. *War and Moral Discourse.* Richmond: John Knox Press, 1969.

Priest, J. "Testament of Moses." In *The Old Testament Pseudepigrapha*, vol. 1, ed. J. H. Charlesworth, 919–934. Garden City, NY: Doubleday & Co., 1983.

Prochsch, Otto. "ἅγιος." In *Theological Dictionary of the New Testament*, vol. 1. Ed. Gerhard Kittel. Translated by Geoffery W. Bromiley. Grand Rapids: Wm. B. Eerdmans, 1974.

Purvis, J. D. "Samaritan Traditions on the Death of Moses." In *Studies on the Testament of Moses*, SBLSCS 4, ed. G. W. E. Nickelsburg. Cambridge, MA: SBL, 1973.

Reddish, Mitchell G., ed. *Apocalyptic Literature: A Reader*. Nashville: Abingdon Press, 1990.

Reicke, Bo. *The Epistles of James, Peter and Jude*. Anchor Bible 37. Garden City, NY: Doubleday, 1964.

Reid, Marty, "Images of the Church in the General Epistles." In *The People of God: Essays on the Believers' Church*. Ed. Paul Basden and David Dockery. Nashville: Broadman Press, 1991.

Rengstorf, Karl H. "δεσπότης, οἰκοδεσπότης, οἰκοδεσποτέω." In *Theological Dictionary of the New Testament*, vol. 2. Ed. Gerhard Kittel. Translated by Geoffrey W. Bromiley. Grand Rapids: Wm. B. Eerdmans, 1964.

Rhoads, D. M. "The Assumption of Moses and Jewish History: 4 B.C.–A.D. 48. In *Studies in the Testament of Moses*, ed. G. W. E. Nickelsburg. SBLSCS 4. Cambridge, MA: SBL, 1973.

Roberts, Alexander, and James Donaldson, eds. *The Ante-Nicene Fathers*, 10 vols. Rev. A. Cleveland Coxe. Reprint of the Edinburgh Edition. Grand Rapids: Wm. B. Eerdmans, 1985.

Robinson, John A. T. *Redating the New Testament*. London: SCM Press, 1976.

Rowland, Christopher. *The Open Heaven: A Study of Apocalyptic in Judaism and Early Christianity*. London: SPCK, 1982.

Rowley, Harold H. *The Relevance of Apocalyptic: A Study of Jewish and Christian Apocalypses from Daniel to Revelation*. London: Lutterworth Press, 1947.

Rowston, Douglas J. "The Most Neglected Book in the New Testament." *New Testament Studies* 21 (1974–75): 554–563.

_____. "The Setting of the Letter of Jude". Ph.D diss., The Southern Baptist Theological Seminary, 1971.

Russell, David S. *Apocalyptic: Ancient and Modern*. London: SCM, 1978.

_____. *Divine Disclosure: An Introduction to Jewish Apocalyptic*. London: SCM, 1992.

_____. *The Method and Message of Jewish Apocalyptic 200 B.C. to A.D. 100*. London: SCM, 1964.

_____. *Old Testament Pseudepigrapha: Prophets and Patriarchs in Early Judaism*. London: SCM Press, 1987.

Saldarini, Anthony J. "Apocalypses and 'Apocalyptic' in Rabbinic Literature." *Semeia* 14 (1979):187–206.

Sanders, E. P. "Testament of Abraham." In *The Old Testament Pseudepigrapha*, vol. 1. Ed. J. H. Charlesworth. Garden City, NY: Doubleday, 1983.

146   *Ethical Admonition in the Epistle of Jude*

Schaff, Phillip, ed. *Nicene and Post-Nicene Fathers*, First Series, 14 vols. Wm. B. Eerdmans, 1983.

Schelkle, Karl H. *Die Petrusbriefe, der Judasbrief*, HTKNT 13/2. Freiburg, Basel, Vienna: Herder, 1961.

Schweizer, Eduard. "The Son of Man." *Journal of Biblical Literature* 79 (1960): 119–129.

_____. "The Son of Man Again." *New Testament Studies* 9 (1962–63): 256–261.

Sellin, G. "Die Häretiker des Judasbriefes." *Zeitschrift für die neutestamentliche Wissenschaft* 77 (1986): 206–225.

Sidebottom, E. M. *James, Jude and 2 Peter*. New Century Bible. London: Thomas Nelson, 1967.

Sider, Robert D., ed. *Collected Works of Erasmus*, 86 vols. Toronto: University of Toronto Press, 1993.

Soards, Marion L. "1 Peter, 2 Peter, and Jude as Evidence for a Petrine School." In *Aufstieg und Niedergang der Römischen Welt*, vol. 2/25/5, ed. W. Hasse, 3827–3849. Berlin/New York: de Gruyter, 1988.

Stassen, Glen. "Critical Variables in Christian Social Ethics." In *Issues in Christian Christian Ethics*, ed. Paul D. Simmons, 57–76. Nashville: Broadman Press, 1980.

_____. "A Social Theory Model for Religious Social Ethics." *The Journal of Religious Ethics* 5 (Spring 1977): 9–37.

Stone, M. E. "Lists of Revealed Things in the Apocalyptic Literature." In *Magnalia Dei: The Mighty Acts of God*. Ed. F. M. Cross, W. E. Lemke, P. D. Miller, Jr. Garden City, NY: Doubleday, 1976.

_____. "Three Armenian Accounts of the Death of Moses." In *Studies on the Testament of Moses*, SBLSCS 4, ed. G. W. E. Nickelsburg, 118–121. Cambridge, MA: SBL, 1973.

Streeter, Burnett H. *The Primitive Church*. London: Macmillan, 1929.

Tatford, Fredk. A. *Jude's Apostates: An Exposition of the Epistle of Jude*. Eastbourne, Sussex: Upperton Press, 1975.

Taylor, Vincent. "The Message of the Epistles: Second Peter and Jude." *Expository Times* 45 (1933–34): 437–441.

Tödt, Heinz Eduard. *The Son of Man In the Synoptic Tradition*. Translated by D. M. Barton. Philadelphia: Westminster Press, 1965.

Tromp, Johannes. *The Assumption of Moses: A Critical Edition with Commentary*. New York: E.J. Brill, 1993.

Tuckett, Christopher. "The Present Son of Man." *Journal for the Study of the New Testament* 14 (1982): 58–81.

_____. "Recent Work on the Son of Man." *Scripture Bulletin* 12 (1981): 14–18.

Tupper, E. Frank. "The Revival of Apocalyptic in Biblical and Theological Studies." *Review and Expositor* 72 (1975): 279–303.

VanderKam, James C. *Enoch and the Growth of an Apocalyptic Tradition*. Catholic Biblical Quarterly Monograph Series, 16. Washington: Catholic Biblical Association, 1984.

_____. "The Theophany of Enoch 1:3b–7, 9." *Vetus Testamentum* 23 (1973): 129–150.

Vermes, Geza. *Jesus and the World of Judaism*. Philadelphia: Fortress Press, 1984.

_____. *Jesus the Jew*. New York: McMillan Press, 1974.

_____. "The Present State of the 'Son of Man' Debate." *Journal of Jewish Studies* 29 (1978): 123–34.

_____. "The Son of Man Debate." *Journal for the Study of the New Testament* 1 (1978): 19–32.

_____. "The Use of *bar nash / bar nasha* in Jewish Aramaic." In *An Aramaic Approach to the Gospels and Acts*, by Matthew Black. 3rd ed., Appendix E. Oxford: Clarendon Press, 1967.

Vögtle, Anton. *Der Judasbrief, Der Zweite Petrusbrief*. Evangelisch-Katholischer Kommentar zum Neuen Testament, 22. Düsseldorf: Benziger; Neukirchen-Vluyn: Neukirchener Verlag, 1994.

Vorster, W. S. "1 Enoch and the Jewish Literary Setting of the New Testament: A Study in Text Types." In *Studies in 1 Enoch and the New Testament: Proceedings of the 19th Meeting of the New Testament Society of South Africa. Neotestamentica* 17 (1983): 1–14.

Walker, William O. "The Son of Man Question and the Synoptic Problem." *New Testament Studies* 28 (1982): 374–388.

_____. "The Son of Man: Some Recent Developments." *Catholic Biblical Quarterly* 45 (1983): 584–607.

Wand, John W. C. *The General Epistles of St. Peter and St. Jude*. Westminster Commentaries. London: Methuen, 1934.

Watson, Duane F. *Invention, Arrangement, and Style: Rhetorical Criticism of Jude and 2 Peter*. SBLDS 104. Atlanta: Scholars Press, 1988.

Whallon, W. "Should We Keep, Omit, or Alter the OI in Jude 12?" *New Testament Studies* 34 (1988): 156–159.

Wheaton, David H. "Jude." In *New Bible Commentary*, ed. David Guthrie. London: Inter-Varsity Press, 1970.

Wilcox, M. "Text Form." In *It is Written: Scripture Citing Scripture: Essays in Honor of Barnabas Lindars SSF*, ed. D. A. Carson and H. G. M. Williamson, 193–294. Cambridge: Cambridge University Press, 1988.

Wilder, Amos N. "The Rhetoric of Ancient and Modern Apocalyptic." *Interpretation* 25 (1971): 436–453.

Wisse, Frederik. "The Epistle of Jude in the History of Heresiology." In *Essays in the Nag Hammadi Texts in Honor of A. Böhlig*, ed. M. Krause, 133–143. Leiden: Brill, 1972.

Wolthius, Thomas. "Jude and Jewish Traditions." *Calvin Theological Journal* 22 (1987): 21–41.

_____. "Jude and the Rhetorician: A Dialogue on the Rhetorical Nature of the Epistle of Jude." *Calvin Theological Journal* 24 (1989): 126–134.

Wright, Norman T. *The Climax of the Covenant: Christ and the Law in Pauline Thought*. Edinburgh: T & T Clark, 1991.

_____. *The New Testament and the People of God*. London: SPCK, 1992.

Zahn, Theodor. *Introduction to the New Testament*, vol. 2. Translated by M. W. Jacobus et al. Edinburgh: T & T Clark, 1909.

Subject Index

Studies in Biblical Literature

This series invites manuscripts from scholars in any area of biblical literature. Both established and innovative methodologies, covering general and particular areas in biblical study, are welcome. The series seeks to make available studies which will make a significant contribution to the ongoing biblical discourse. Scholars who have interests in gender and sociocultural hermeneutics are particularly encouraged to consider this series.

For further information about the series and for the submission of manuscripts, contact:

Hemchand Gossai
Department of Philosophy and Religion
Culver-Stockton College
Canton, MO 63435